Sendai ● Sendai

Tokyo ● Tokyo

Sendai city: Northeastern region of Japan, 280 km from Tokyo (3 hours by train).
Population: 1.015.253 (1 April 2003 est.). Government center of Tohoku region.

Sendai Mediatheque

verB
monograph

Sendai Mediatheque

Under construction
Toyo Ito

The Mediatheque concept

Looking back on the 1995 Sendai Mediatheque competition, it still stands as an altogether unusual event in the history of open competitions in Japan. One unique aspect is that, more than a distinctive expression as a building per se, what was sought was a whole new building "type" (typology). Another peculiarity was the uncompromising transparency and openness of the competition itself.

The Sendai Mediatheque was, in the very first planning stages, conceived as an amalgam of four different programs: a new building for the Sendai Civic Gallery whose lease period was coming to term (it was previously housed in a space rented within a department store), a replacement structure for the delapidated Aoba-ku Branch of the Sendai Public Library, improvements in the Sendai Audiovisual Learning Center, and the necessity for an information services center for the audiovisually impaired.

In order to firm up design competition criteria by which to choose an architect for the Mediatheque, as well as to sort out the various programmatic complexities from a specialist perspective, the City of Sendai entrusted a research team headed by Professor Sugano at the Architectural Faculty, Tohoku University, Sendai, with the task of drawing up competition guidelines. What resulted were the following six aspects of consideration:

1. Multifunctionality: all the required institutional functions had to fit within one compact 4000 m^2 site secured on Jozenji-dori Avenue in the heart of the city.

2. Art: not merely a large space to hold ongoing regional exhibitions, but also a workshop section with full-time curators, as well as a media center fully equipped to handle the demands of digital-age multimedia.

3. Data media (books): in addition to present library functions, offering integrated services of audiovisual materials (ultimately inclusive of even artworks), as well as on-line networking capabilities. Not merely a space for looking at "books," but a place for searching out "information."

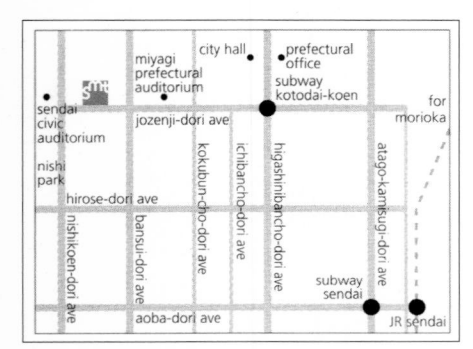

Access map from the JR Sendai station

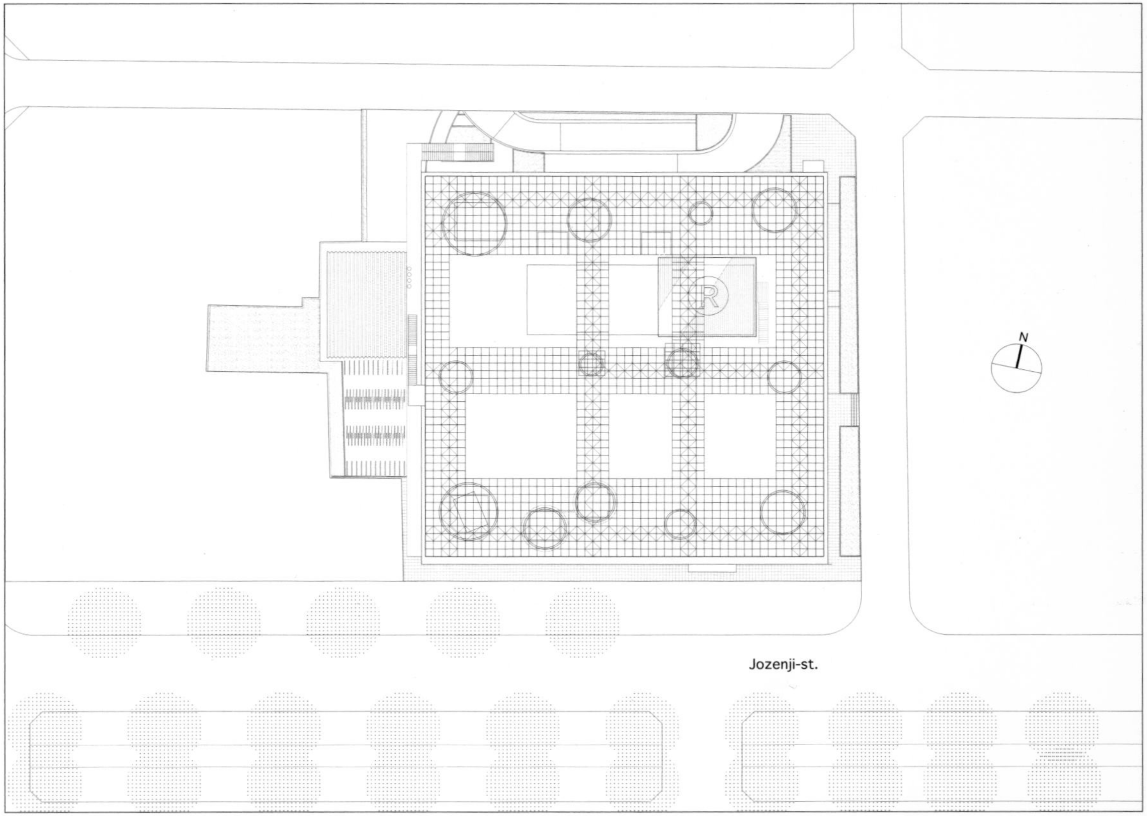

Site plan

Jozenji-st.

Idea

Under
construction

4. Operations: unification of previously separate operations in order to realize improved services, rational use of available space, and reduced compartmentalization.

5. Urbanism: a key project in the shaping of the 21st-century city, intended to put Sendai proudly on the world map. Also, conceived as a leavening agent to liven up the existing district around the site.

6. Design competition: in order to make a clean sweep of various problems caused by lack of transparency in recent institutional projects initiated by administrations, the architect is to be selected by highly transparent and open methods. (From the Sendai Mediatheque Design Competition Records.)

From this we can see that even prior to the launch of the competition, this was to be no conventional facility. Likewise in the design competition application guidelines, the Mediatheque is defined as "the image of a new urban function space for a new age, which together with collectively amassing and providing sensual media such as art, intellectual media such as books and other data sources, as well as new media such as electronic audiovisuals that are a fusion of these, will also support each individual citizen in realizing his or her imaginative potential to communicate." Thus, from the very top of the guidelines, the task is set at nothing less than the pursuit of an archetype.

The facility to be known as the Mediatheque is not without precedents, albeit few, in the West. Particularly noteworthy are the German model, ZKM in Karlsruhe, dedicated to research fusing art and digital technology, as well as to the cultivation of media artists; and the French model, the Carré d'Art in Nimes, centered on a library yet aspiring to fuse art and data media.

The Sendai approach might seem close to the latter, though in any case it is no mere civic culture meeting hall. The call that went out under the rubric of `Mediatheque´, inclusive of any programatic reworking, was to prove a decisive event for the developments to come:

"A facility whose infrastructure of present day information technology composes a sum intellectual mass, such as may also be used to create new emblematic ideas.... a civic facility aimed at promoting arts and culture and lifelong learning, not by present standards of service, but by supporting participatory, self-expressive activities."

From the application guidebook for the competition

Jury statement

The role of jury members in a design competition for an institutional project is to represent and support the public administration as a client on one hand, and the citizens as the building's users on the other. These are the premises that should guide the selection of an architect or of a particular competition entry by a group of outsiders — either specialists in architectural design or in the specific facilities to be judged. But in recent years there have been several examples of unfair selection according to political considerations or interests. In the competition for the Sendai Mediatheque (tentative name), we would like to make a clear statement as a judging committee regarding the actual concerns of this project and to make the selection clear and fair.

1. Selection process
- The jury is composed of specialists who evaluate the contents of the proposals and their architectural solutions.
- The jury will interview the authors of a first selection of the best proposals, and will choose one single team or 'person' to execute the basic design or 'idea'.
- The selection process must be open to the public, especially the final stage, which could be broadcasted live.

2. Judging standards
- The Mediatheque, in its existing conceptual framework, is a complex facility including an art gallery, a public library, audiovisual services, etc. But here, the term should be understood in a broader sense as a media facility for receiving and transmitting information, which is supposed to be used by a diversity of citizens in a diversity of ways. Thus, we expect positive proposals regarding the contents of the program, allowing for the meeting and information exchange among citizens and for the space to be open to the city.
- Obviously, design excellency will also be evaluated, aspiring to the production of an original architype that will respond to the requirements of new media.

September 1994
Arata Isozaki, President of the jury

A "place" structured by tubes and plates

The aim of our proposal as selected was, in a sense, a simple prototypical building. By prototypical, I mean to say not a specific form of building attuned to one set specific program, but rather a system capable of meeting any and all programatic conditions that might arise. Now that the construction is completed, the building does indeed embody such flexibility, yet is far different in character from the so-called 20th-century ideal of "universal space."

The Sendai Mediatheque is comprised of three basic architectural elements: plates (floors), tubes (columns), and skin (facade/exterior walls).

All buildings stripped of extraneous elements reduce down to the fundamental roof plus the structure of walls, columns and floors. However, in most cases these make up a specific compound volume designed to meet a given function, hence they remain ordinary particularized forms. In the Sendai Mediatheque, however, from its very first conception we pursued a structural system of only the above three elements — or to put it even more extremely, of only plates (floor slabs) and tubes (columns). This shows quite plainly in the early sketches. Even in the competition-stage model, the proposed building was highly abstract, with all but these three elements pared away.

Of course, in order to make this a real building to be used it was necessary to add on many other elements: exterior walls to separate inside from out, not to mention numerous partition wall, doors, elevators, stairways... In the building as actually constructed, the additional elements are many. So perhaps the realized building is no longer prototypical and thus no different from other buildings. Certainly the building-in-the-making is not as abstract as the competition model.

Nonetheless, over the last five years our team has tirelessly continued to do studies imaged upon strictly abstract tube-and-plate models. These studies have, in other words, been an exercise in how to maintain the protypical image even while adding on elements.

Modernist architecture can be said to have proposed two schemes of prototypical building: Mies van der Rohe's "universal space" and Le Corbusier's Domino system. The former is an articulated space composed

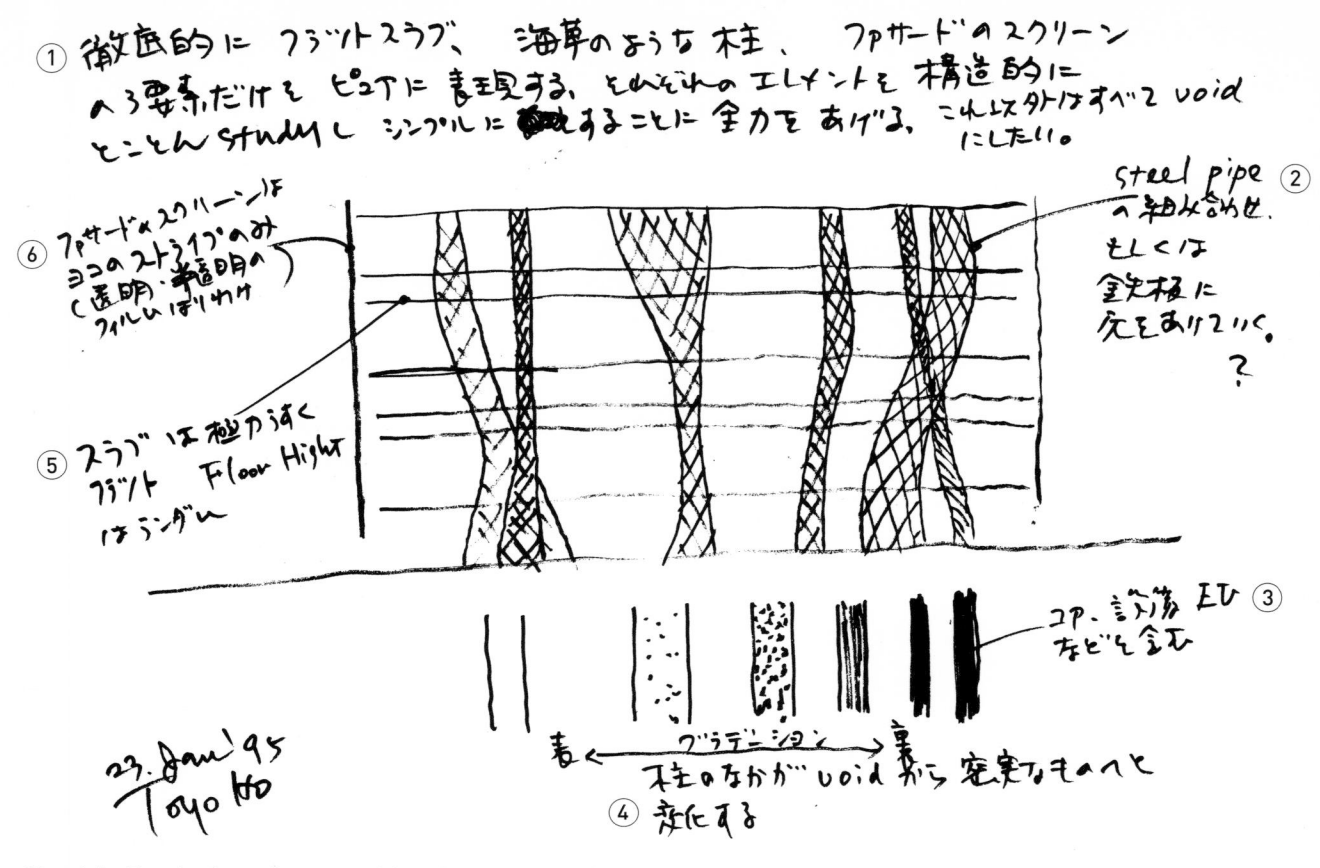

① 徹底的に フラットスラブ、 海草のような柱、 ファサードのスクリーン
　の3要素だけを ピュアに 表現する、 それぞれの エレメントを 構造的に
　とことん study し シンプルに 構成することに 全力を あげる、 これ以外はすべて void
　にしたい。

⑥ ファサードのスクリーンは　　　　　　　　　　　　　　　　　　　② steel pipe
　ヨコのストライプのみ　　　　　　　　　　　　　　　　　　　　　　の軸X組み合せ、
　（透明・半透明の　　　　　　　　　　　　　　　　　　　　　　　　もしくは
　フィルムばりかけ　　　　　　　　　　　　　　　　　　　　　　　　鉄板に
　　　　　　　　　　　　　　　　　　　　　　　　　　　　　　　　　穴をあけていく。

⑤ スラブは極力うすく　　　　　　　　　　　　　　　　　　　　　　？
　フラット　Floor Hight
　はランダム

　　　　　　　　　　　　　　　　　　　　　　　　　　③ コア・設備 及び
　　　　　　　　　　　　　　　　　　　　　　　　　　などを含む

　　　　　　　　表←　グラデーション　→裏
　　　　　　　柱のなかが void から 密実なものへと
　　　　　④ 変化する

23. Jan '95
Toyo Ito

Sketch by Toyo Ito from the competition phase • 1 complete flat slab, seaweed-like columns, screen façade, express only these three elements in the purest way, study each element structurally, and simplify them as much as possible, all the rest is left as a void **• 2** crossed steel pipe, or punch-holes on steel plate **• 3** include circulation cores or fitting **• 4** front--gradation--back content of the columns varies from void to dense **• 5** thinnest slab, random floor height **• 6** screen façade has only horizontal strips (with transparent or translucent film)

Idea

Under
construction

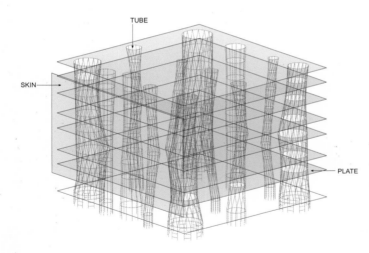

TUBE

SKIN →

← PLATE

'Domino' construction system of Sendai Mediatheque.
It consists of three elements: plate, tube and skin.

of a uniform three-dimensional gridwork of posts and beams, more or less adopted in all high-rise office buildings today, indefinitely extendible in principle both vertically and horizontally; the latter is composed of columns and flat slabs without beams. If Mies' space is all glass and steel in image, Le Corbusier's is concrete. The construction system we proposed for the Sendai Mediatheque perhaps resembles the Domino in its use of flat slabs and columns, but whereas Le Corbusier's chosen material was concrete, the Sendai floors are "honeycomb slabs," twin steel plates with ribbing spaced in between, which allows for a far broader span than concrete. Moreover, the columns are hollow bundles of steel pipes, each with its own tubular shape ranging in diameter from 2m to 9m. And while each of these tubes is circular in cross-section, the centers shift from top to bottom so that they thread between floors at an angle. By no means organic forms, yet each tends toward its own individuated expression. These various hollow tubes serve as vertical transports and energy core connections, housing elevators, stairways, ducts and cables. Glass-covered tube serve as air-supply and exhaust flues, while also conducting natural light down to the lower levels. Within this stratified man-made environment, the tubes function as conduits for the natural elements of light and air.

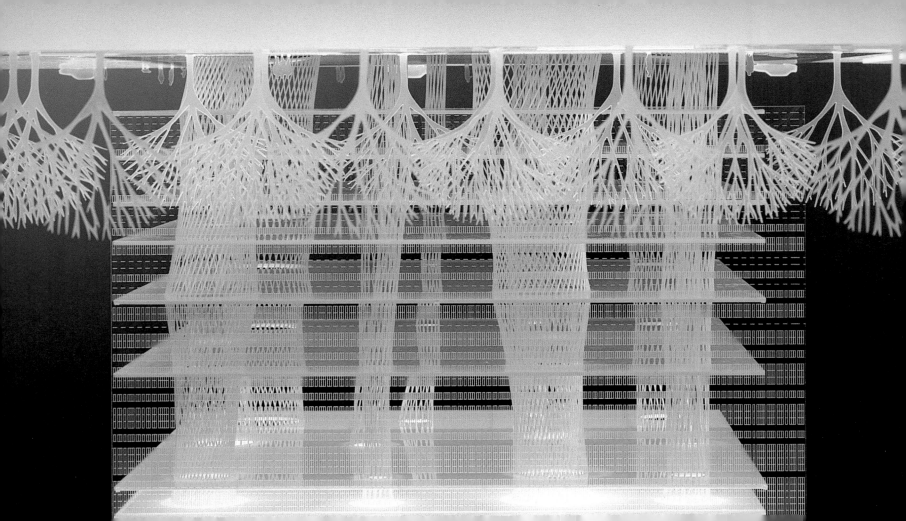

Idea

● Under
construction

Another feature of our system is an almost random placement of the tubes in plan and the varying floor heights for each floor. The intent here is not necessarily toward an industrial productivity or spatial uniformity as with Le Corbusier or Mies, but rather toward a site-specific uniqueness as seen in the treatment of the tubes. In fact, we had originally envisioned running the ribs through the 50 m^2 honeycomb floor at regular 1m grid intervals, but as planning progressed it became clear that the distribution of force around the tubes and in middle of the floors differed too greatly, so the ribs were made to radiate out from the tubes. The result is that the distribution of force is not uniform throughout the slabs, so different spaces have different dynamics, a clear indication via structural analyses of the specifications of the various spaces on each floor. Introducing the tubes made the floors non-uniform, causing a ripple effect, which brings a fluidity to the spaces.

The spatial experience is not unlike walking through the woods. The presence of trees creates different spaces among which people can choose where to do whatever, in much the same way as humans since ancient times have made places to live within the flux of nature. Long ago, the act of making a building used to consist in creating relationships relative to this natural flux, but architecture has long since cut itself off from such fluidity and turned into a labor of linking up closed rooms. But the body feels stifled when sealed inside such static rooms.

Our greatest hope for a multilevel scheme such as Sendai is to create "differentiated spatialities." Designating "room" spaces specific to isolated functions is to limit free action, whereas human actions are originally complex in nature and should not be specified one particular action to one particular space. To assign such single-definition correspondences is modernist planification. With the Sendai Mediatheque, we do not unilaterally assign "room" spaces or specify particular uses; rather we want the building to allow users to discover new places and new uses for themselves. Shouldn't a new public building truly invite discovery and a little creativity? Our efforts to make each tube different properly aspired to creating an architecture that would allow such "discovery of places."

Even now after the opening, activities to be conducted here at the Sendai Mediatheque are still open to discussion, which we'd like to think has something to do with our all-out avoidance of "rooms." Of course, it goes without saying that there are spaces that must be enclosed in order to function. However, compared to the normal public building, Sendai has dramatically fewer closed-off "rooms," all made possible by the intervening tubes. These five years, as each floor has continued to evolve, we've drawn an incredible number of floor plans. All of them are quite abstract, square-framed diagrams on which the activities for each floor are indicated only in brief symbolic notation. They almost look like gameboards where the markings show a game in play. Unlike the typical floor plan completely constrained by established practices, these Sendai floor plans seem to function a bit more freely. Whether or not the game will continue past the completion of the building is anyone's guess.

The third element of the building, the skin, forms a huge screen over three of the five outer surfaces (four walls plus roof). The main facade facing onto the zelkova trees of Jozenji-dori Avenue is covered in a double-paned glass screen (double skin), affixed with a pattern of horizontal stripes as per the original design so as to create subtle visual effects between the exterior and interior and change the appearance of the building continuously throughout the day, as light reflects or passes through the two layers of glass. The roof and west side are covered in metal-louvered screens, both temporary-looking, almost like lightweight screens floating off the volume of the building itself. The east and north sides vary materials with each floor, the spaces between the slabs filled with transparent and semi-transparent glass or metal as expressions of the use-related treatment of the interiors extended outside, though unlike the other three sides this probably seems to directly expose the insides of the skin.

Together, these various skin surfacings give the building overall a presence quite distinct to any previous architecture. The reason seems to be that we have tried to see the building in a way diametrically opposite to the usual single-volumetric expression based on a cosmology of architectural self-containment. Instead, using the given 50m-square site, we have cut away a 36m high cube from the space of the city and exposed the volume in cross-section.

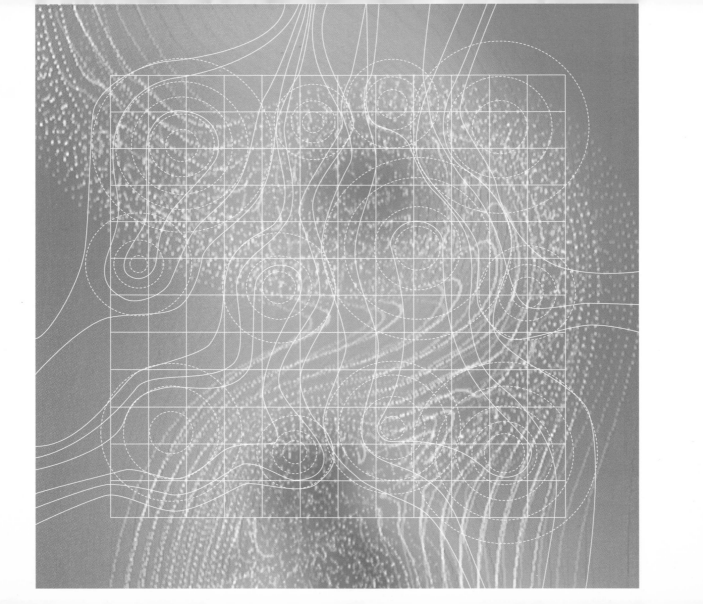

Plan studies, competition stage • 1F: permanent exhibition of contemporary art (barrier free) by means of light, sound, video (image of ripples) • **2F:** workshop, terrace, office, entrance hall, shop, cafe, information, toilet • **3F:** general/children's open-stack reading room, reference room for newspapers and magazines, image of water flow (media stream), terrace, synapse • **4F:** bookshelves and reading room facing outside, strong light suggests directions, memory • **5F:** audiovisual meeting space, video media, library, processing and sending, ripples of information, sit at the terminals, island, devices • **6F:** art program exhibition room, storage, service, circulation, random pattern • **7F:** complete free space, installation, platform

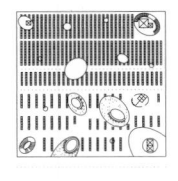
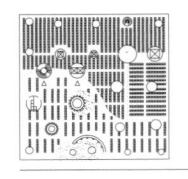
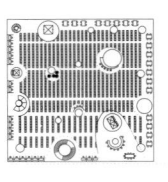
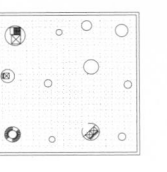 7th floor

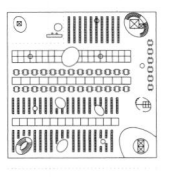
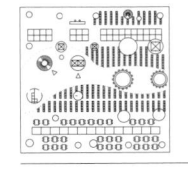

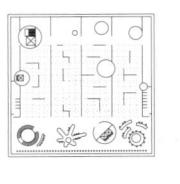 6th floor

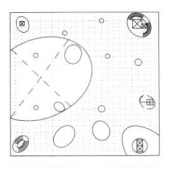
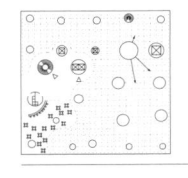
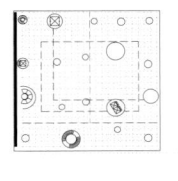
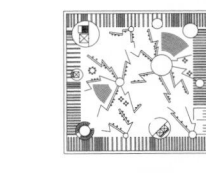 5th floor

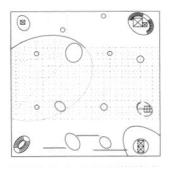
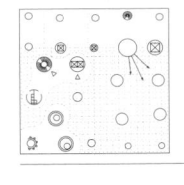
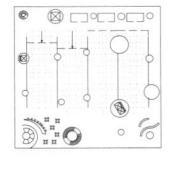
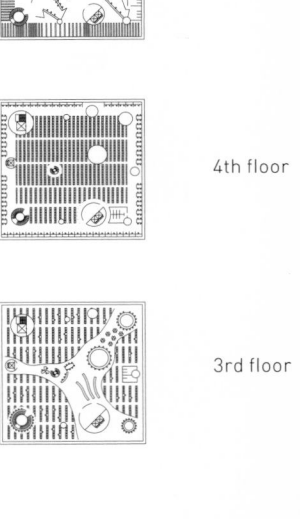 4th floor

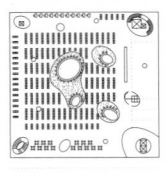
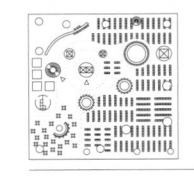
 3rd floor

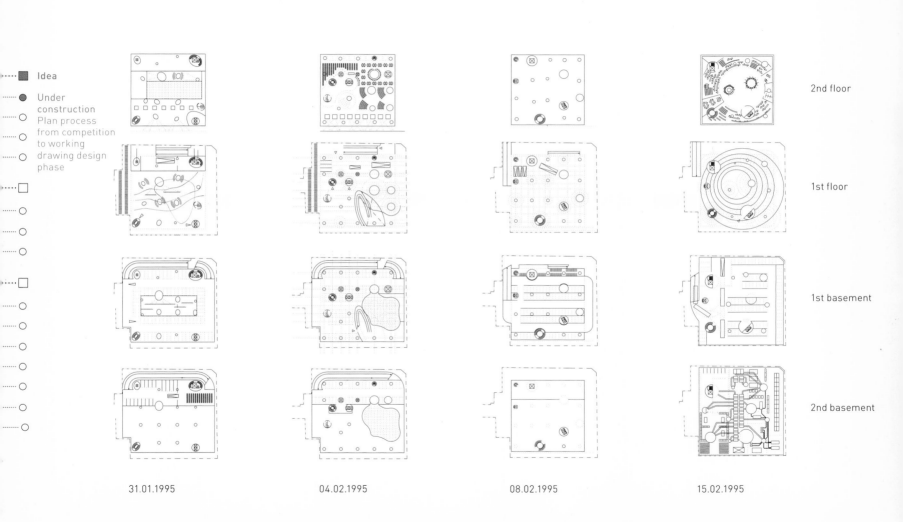

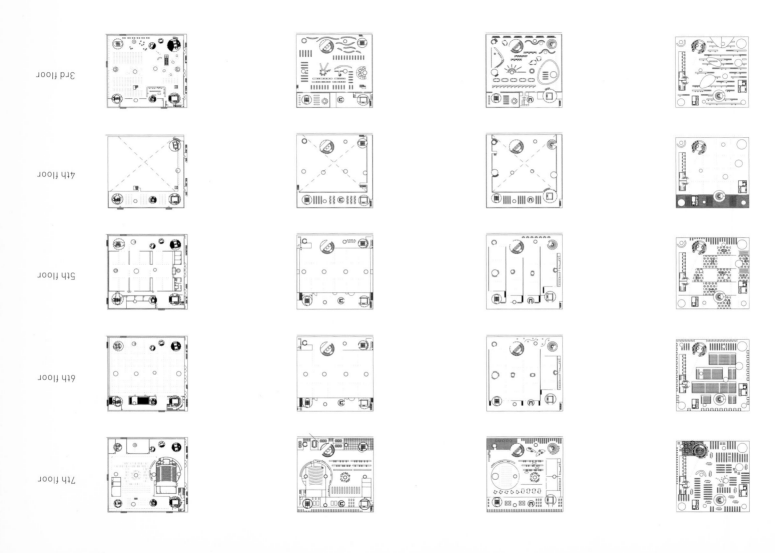

3rd floor

4th floor

5th floor

6th floor

7th floor

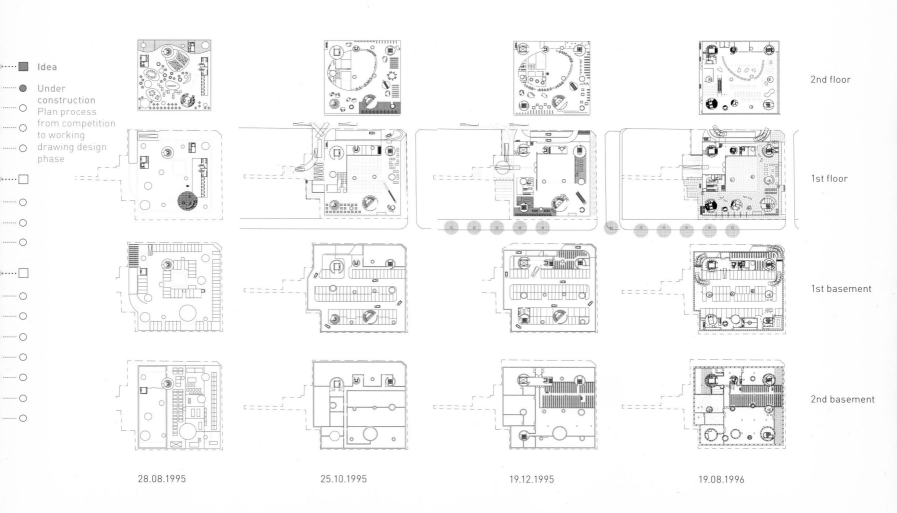

Idea

Under construction
Plan process from competition to working drawing design phase

2nd floor

1st floor

1st basement

2nd basement

28.08.1995   25.10.1995   19.12.1995   19.08.1996

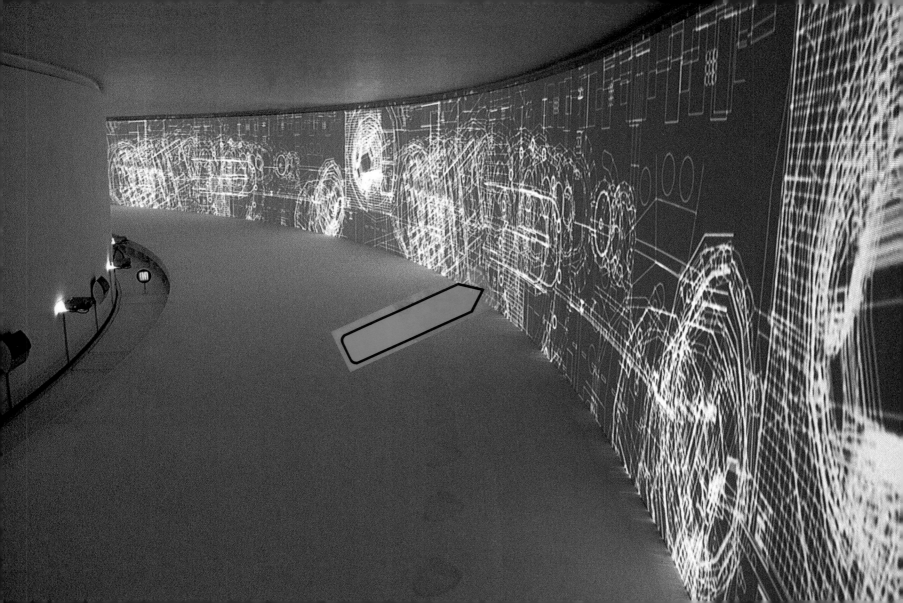

Idea

Under
construction

Blurring Architecture

From late autumn 1999 to the beginning of 2000, our exhibition *Blurring Architecture* was held simulta-neously in Aachen, Germany, and Tokyo (the Aachen exhibition at the Suermondt-Ludwig-Museum from October to January, the Tokyo exhibition at TN Probe from November to December), and then at deSingel, Antwerp, and the Louisiana Musem of Modern Art near Copenhagen. An installation using computer-graphic simulations of the Sendai Mediatheque was created for the exhibition.

"Blurring" was perhaps not the right word, at least not in the usual sense of haziness or indistinct vision. So why then this title for an exhibition about the Sendai Mediatheque? Simply put, it was because the facility aimed to be "barrier free", here taken in the broadest sense of the word. Not merely in terms of the physical problems faced by the handicapped (as in the Mediatheque charter), but also in terms of problems of mutual interpenetrability between divergent programs — not to mention the barriers set up by architecture itself.

As we have already mentioned, public buildings today are typically a series of subdivided and self-con-tained "rooms," all the easier to control and maintain specialized functions for being closed-in. Opening up ambiguous thresholds only makes things that much more difficult to manage. And not just "rooms" — the same goes for "buildings" as units. As a result, the contemporary city is a lineup of sealed boxes with mutually unrelated, context-less exteriors. Even the shapes of public spaces and residential envi-ronments are merely the result of ruthlessly cutting off independent, enclosed interiors from the world outside. "Blurring" thus also referred to our attempts at a looser and more open ambiguity between inside and out.

In Sendai we had tubes penetrating the floors. Where in an ordinary office building there would be no relationships between up and down, the introduction of tubes gives a visual intimation of other floors as well as serving as mutually connecting vertical traffic spaces. They make for a degree of interpenetrabil-ity between floors, what we might term a "blurring" of levels.

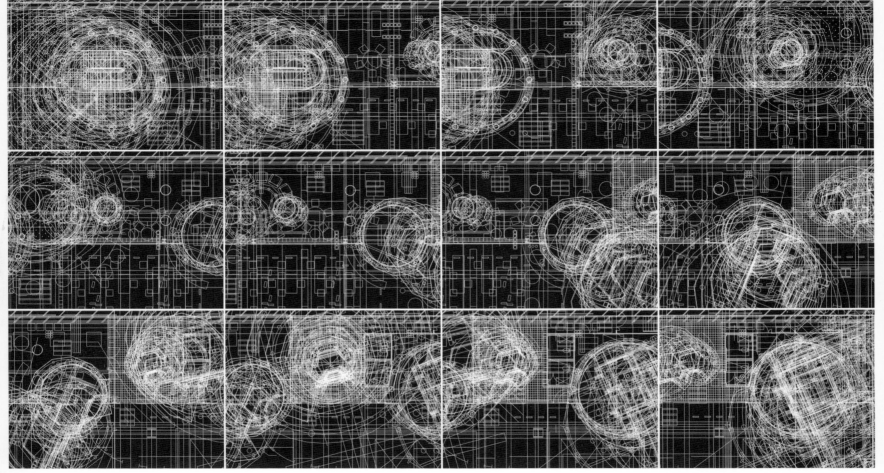

Toyo Ito: Blurring Architecture
Projection sequence of overlapped floor plans

Idea

Under
construction

In both exhibition spaces, computer simulations of Sendai were shown in four large-screen video projections. These black and white CG images were "collages" of plans we'd drawn up over the last few years in the process of realizing the building, running studies that changed minutely over repetition, forming a series of overlapping floor plans that could be projected sequentially. The study process was thus compressed in time and displayed as a kind of graphic sign notation. The forest of tubes, cut into cross-section and elevation, appeared in the video projection to flow endlessly in both vertical and horizontal directions. All were abstractions of the spatial experience of the building, depicting the Sendai Mediatheque free of spatial and temporal thresholds, yet another sense of "blurring."

At the Tokyo exhibition, alongside these CG screens were monitors showing hundreds of digital images of the building site. The actual site was a raw struggle with steel, the very antithesis of the clean, exact world of abstract computer graphics. We had recorded over a year's worth of these metalwork battle scenes. The labors of working the thick, heavy metal, applying the heat of welding torches, beating bent steel plates, cutting and stripping and welding again, iron that would stop at nothing until it was covered with scars: virtually a time-lapse history of primitive civilization since the Iron Age in its fight with physical matter. Matter that can never be more than matter, almost pitiable for its very strength.

The Sendai Mediatheque was thus a space in which these two completely different visions coexisted: the slowly flowing, abstracted sign-space of the huge wall screens, and the metal-grimed matter-scape of the monitors. The steel wars came to an end, but the signifier streams still flow on. The Sendai Mediatheque is now open as a facility; these two diametrically coexistent spaces or not, the "building" has begun to be used and become part of society. Even so, the Mediatheque has already been "in use" these five years. The opening is merely a point of passage in the building's long history. For it still must continue being created, it must go on changing. The Sendai Mediatheque must always remain under construction.

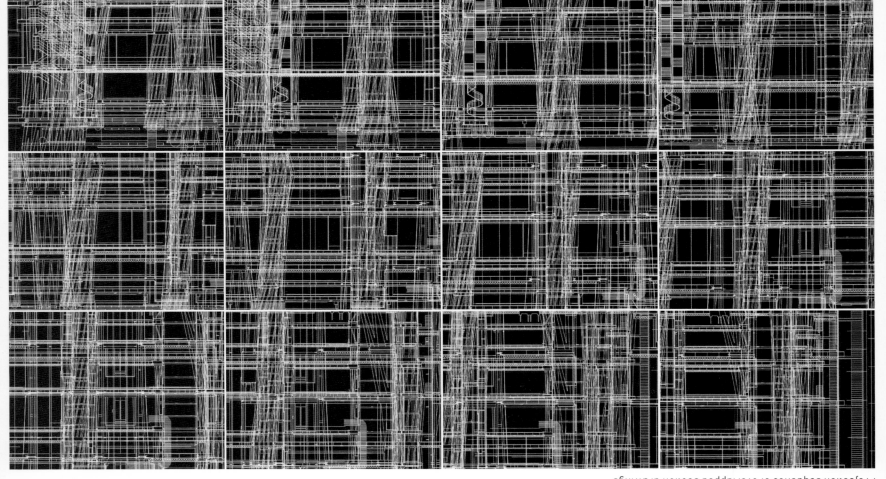

Projection sequence of overlapped section drawings

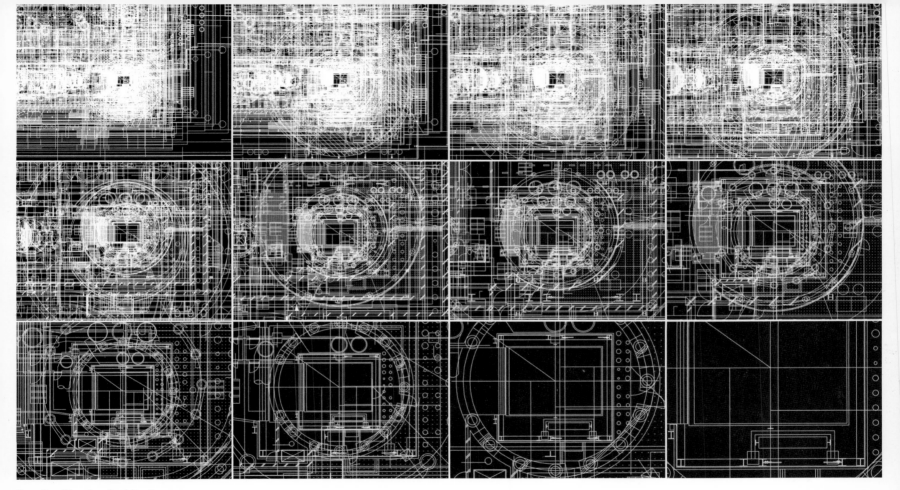

Toyo Ito: Blurring Architecture
Down into the tube. Projection sequence
of overlapped tube detail plans

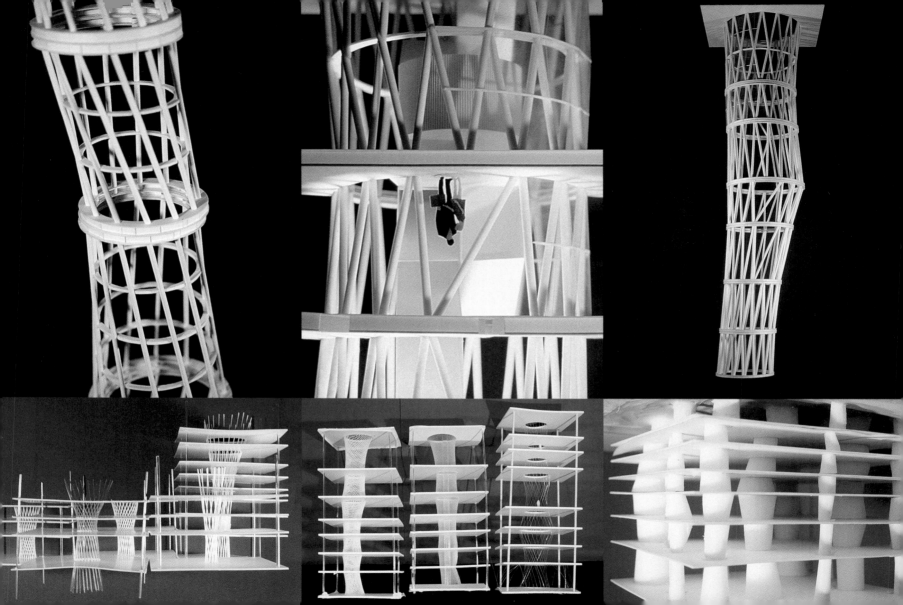

↑ Series of study models of the tubes using various materials
(styrofoam, net, wire, plastic sticks, stocking)

Three principles of Sendai Mediatheque*
Eishi Katsura, library and information specialist, member of the project study committee

1. The Sendai Mediatheque flexibly serves the needs of people by supplying the latest knowledge and culture.
The Sendai Mediatheque is to be a space for the realization of knowledge. 'Latest knowledge and culture' does not mean that only the most advanced information technology will be used, but that it will offer services which can contribute to the growth and development of the Sendai Mediatheque itself, by constantly inverting the position of 'servant' and 'served' spaces. Traditional cultural facilities are systems housing collections which are open to the public, based on the museum and library typologies of the modern era and built for the purpose of educating the public.
As a result, these facilities have been administrated by the governments or their elites, constituted as 'servant' bodies. But it is not necessary here to open a new public facility to support this elite consciousness or the elitism of a 'servant' side. We can instead redirect some of the functions of existing cultural facilities toward pursuing discovery and creation. This new direction means that the Sendai Mediatheque has to acquire a sophisticated nodal structure, providing a succession of services with a flexible or 'elastic' structure. And this requires dismantling the organization principles of traditional facilities such as a library or an art gallery.

2. The Sendai Mediatheque maximizes networking potentials through nodes rather than terminals.
The Sendai Mediatheque proposes a new concept of public facility which enhances activities rather than acting as their servant framework. Existing public facilities define conclusive functions and are managed according to these definitions — reading books (library), appreciating art (museum), viewing plays or listening to concerts (concert hall), etc. If we think for instance of library functions, to read or take out books, it is difficult to fully satisfy them in a single facility, as regular budgets will become insufficient for purchasing all necessary books. Instead, the idea of creating through the Sendai Mediatheque a library consortium together with the university library and other specialized libraries in the region allows us to share acquisitions and data, thus reducing costs. The Mediatheque originates as a 'node' in the library network.

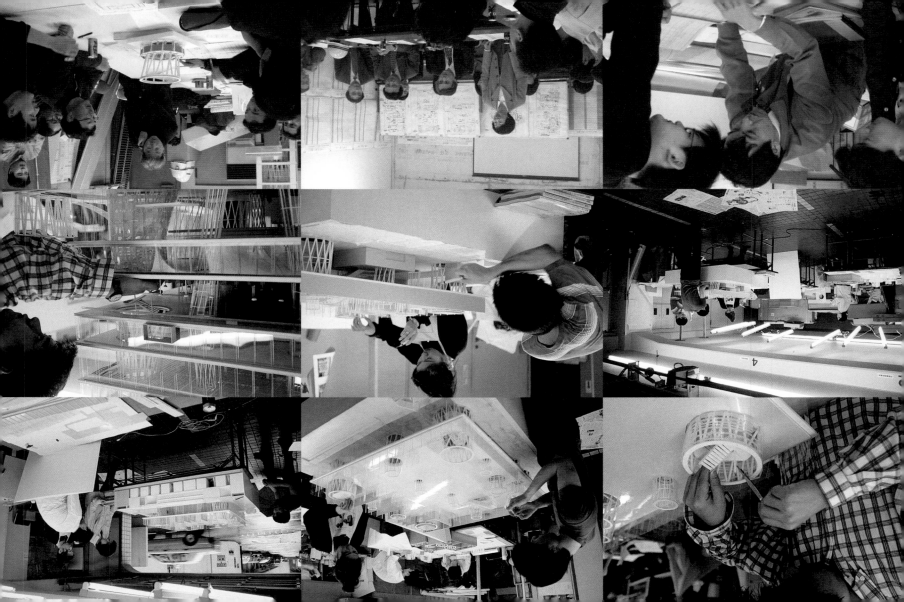

Given that the Mediatheque is a multi-functional facility, we have to take advantage of the amount and diversity of people who come here for various purposes. The workshops become an important project to allow people to come together, to enhance encounters and communication. In this nodal facility, 'collection' becomes 'connection'.

3. The Sendai Mediatheque serves all people including the disabled and people of different languages and cultures by eliminating all barriers.

The Sendai Mediatheque brings together different interests in everyday life. In public space, different interests mean a variety of standpoints, but the Mediatheque is different from a park in the sense that it plays a role in the accumulation of knowledge and know-how, and eventually in the erasure of barriers regarding accessibility, gender, age, or language differences.

The Mediatheque is not a welfare facility, but it accumulates knowledge and know-how that have an impact on welfare. Bringing together different public interests in exhibitions and workshops suggests the orientation of the Mediatheque's role as a node that allows these interests to develop and communicate.

* Excerpt from Eishi Katsura, 'Nodal thought' in *Inter Communication* no. 36.

The making of the Sendai Mediatheque

08.1989	The Arts Association of Miyagi Prefecture asks for the construction of a new museum in Sendai.
01.1992	A bus depot of the transportation authority in Zenjoji Street is selected as the site for the new city gallery.
09.1992	Aoba library (Sendai city library) is added to the project.
03.1993	The committee for the definition of the new city gallery submits a preliminary project plan to the Mayor of Sendai.
02.1994	Wide range of opinions from citizens are collected.
05.1994	The Jozenji Urban policy council presents a petition to the city.
06.1994	The city of Sendai decides to launch an open competition for a new art and cultural complex that includes a new city gallery, library, visual media center, and information center for the vision- or hearing-impaired.
08.1994	The city holds a citizens' meeting to collect their opinions on the project.
09.1994	Launching of the architectural design competition.
03.1995	Toyo Ito & Associates are selected as the architects.
08.1995	First meeting of the Mediatheque Project Exploratory Committee.
10.1995	Opinions from several users' groups are gathered.
11.1995	The citizens' discussion 'Wai wai talk II' is held.
05.1996	Presentation of the Mediatheque Project Exploratory Committee Report.
11.1996	Opinions from several users' groups are gathered again.
12.1996	The first pre-opening event 'The Digital Revolution and its Whereabouts' is held (21 pre-opening events were organized).
10.1997	Selection of construction companies.
11.1997	An explanatory meeting is held for the users' groups.
12.1997	Beginning of construction.
04.1999	The Sendai Mediatheque Preparatory Room is created in the Sendai Community Foundation.
05.1999	Publication of the Mediatheque Preparatory Room magazine no. 1 (continued until no. 19).
11.1999	The architectural seminar 'Where the Sendai Mediatheque is heading' is held at the Tokyo Design Center.
03.2000	The ordinances of the Sendai Mediatheque are established.
08.2000	Building completion.
11.2000	The existing city gallery, library and audiovisual media resource center close down.
12.2000	The city library moves to its new premises.
01.2001	Opening of the Sendai Mediatheque and city library.
01-03.'01	The opening event 'Message / open the door of the words' is held.

2nd floor plan study during construction, 1999

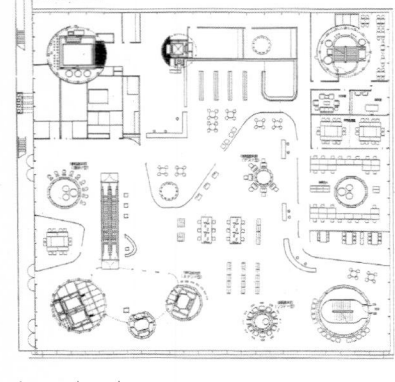

Irregular plan

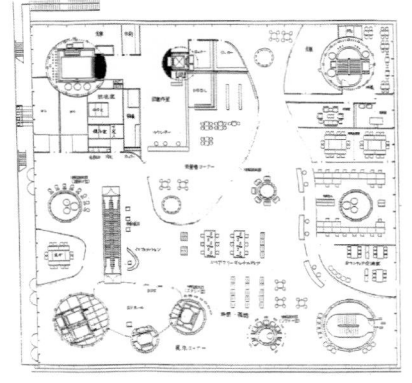

Amoeba plan

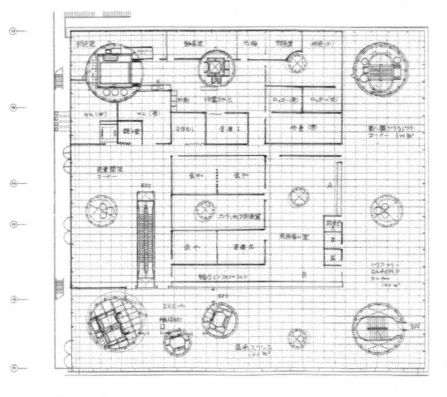

Box plan

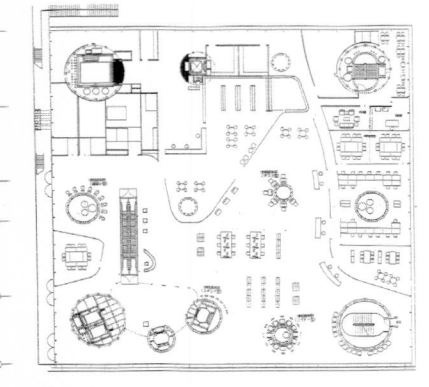

Map plan

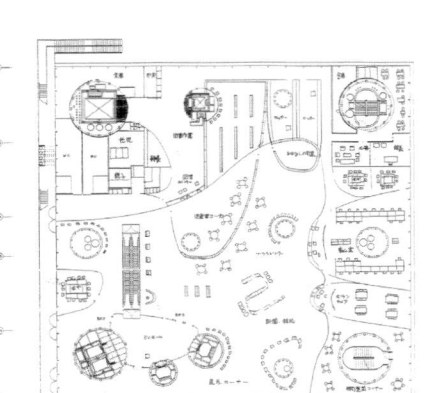

Weather chart plan

Stripe plan

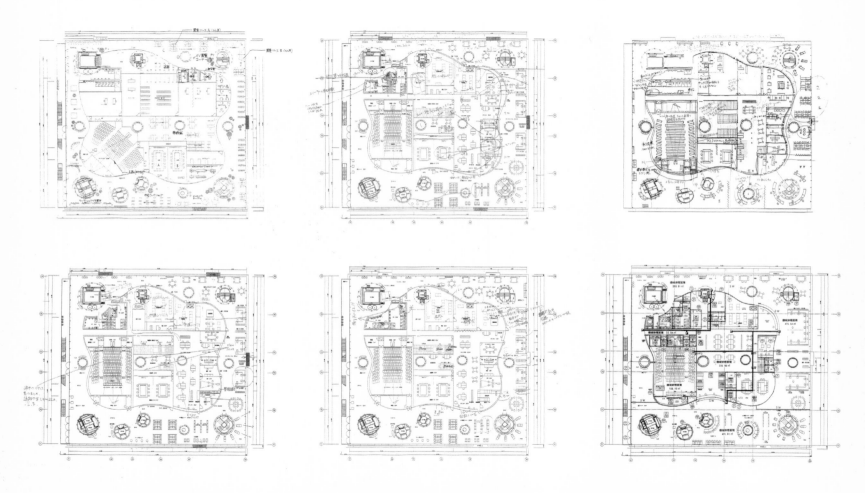

Model construction sequence

Construction process
Illustrations taken from a brochure given to people visiting the construction site

04.1998
Excavating work

07.1998
Building frame foundation work

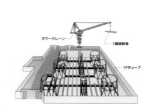

09.1998
Beams and steel-frame assembly, ground floor

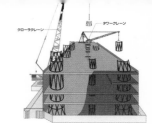

10.1999
Steel-frame tube assembly, 5th floor

12.1999
Assembly of honeycomb plate, roof level

01.2000
Dismantlement of the tower crane

05.2000
Fitting-in of the glass curtain wall

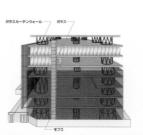

07.2000
Completion

12.05.1998   01.05.1998   17.04.1998   01.04.1998

10.03.1998   03.03.1998   16.02.1998   19.01.1998

Fixed observation point

08.05.1998 10.06.1998 03.07.1998 05.08.1998

19.08.1998 01.10.1998 22.10.1998 04.12.1998

25.11.1999   27.01.2000   15.02.2000   16.03.2000

14.04.2000   02.05.2000   19.05.2000   25.09.2000

Mutsuro Sasaki's study sketch of the geometry of the tubes in the competition phase

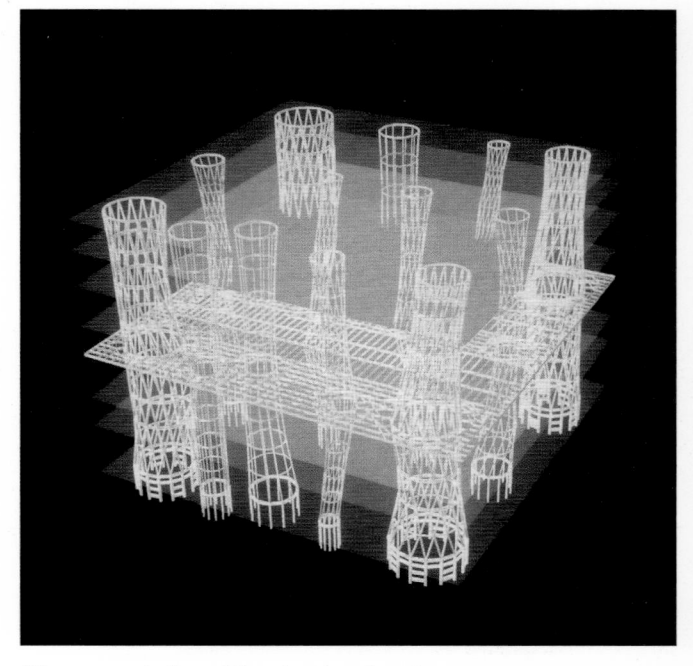

3D representation of the structural system

Structure
Interview with Mutsuro Sasaki and Masahiro Ikeda, structural engineers

Verb: Which role should engineers play in architectural design?

Sasaki: The roles of the architect and of the structural engineer should not be divided, but subject to exchange. At the end of the 19th century, structural engineers were leading modern architecture, as in the case of the Eiffel Tower. Afterwards, architects like Viollet-le-Duc began to pay attention to the importance of engineering, and their ideas would later influence architects like Mies van der Rohe and Le Corbusier. But before then most architects were only dealing with styles; engineers, on the other hand, were the ones trying to be ahead of their time and to correspond to the needs of society. Since the beginning of the 20th century, architects have begun to have a more direct connection to society and their clients, and these roles have changed: architects now undertake such projects, and engineers join them. But even today, architects and engineers still have different types of education and little in common. I think this is a problem, because the two have to be on equal terms — neither should take initiative over the other in the physical creation of architecture.

Verb: In the case of the Sendai Mediatheque, it seems that the two of you started to collaborate from Toyo Ito's very first sketch by exchanging ideas, feeding them back to each other, and so on.

Sasaki: When I first saw Toyo Ito's shocking sketch, I had an intuitive structural idea on how to make the building; it was not so easy to think about how to ¨build¨ it, in terms of the method of construction, the materials, etc. But to tell the truth, I found that my image of this project and his image of it were completely different. He describes the building as a type of Dom-Ino, but for me it was something more like Mies van der Rohe and Gaudí combined. So we had quite different concepts. It could be that the singularity of this building comes from this difference. Generally, engineers try to reach a sort of accommodation with the architects, but there are many excellent exceptions. For example, the most outstanding aspect of the collaboration between Kenzo Tange and Yoshikatsu Tsuboi was that they understood each other, but remained misunderstood at the same time. Similarly in the Kimbell Art Museum project, the

Construction

Structure

way that Louis Kahn thought about the structure was completely different from that of the engineer, August E. Komendant. But these misunderstandings are very interesting. Once in an interview, Toyo Ito was asked, 'Is the Mediatheque predominantly a work of architecture or engineering?', and he answered, 'Both'. (see *Crossing* no. 2, ¨[Ex]changing Roles¨, June 2001) But now I see that if our ways of thinking had been balanced, we could not have merged. It was only possible to unite because we were different, even though we did not intend to be.

Verb: Finally, the tubes do not go through the floors but are cut at each floor, like in the models.

Sasaki: In the end, the tubes are cut into pieces by each floor plate. This is both because it was impossible to carry full-length tubes from the factory to the site, and because the easiest way to fabricate the building was to stack the floor plates on top of tube sections cut to each floor height. At one point we tried to make the tube sections each three floors high and fix the two intermediate floors from the side, but we found that to fix these floors properly it became necessary to remove pieces of the tube at the construction site. So finally we decided to cut the tubes for each floor. Thus we reached the most simple structure — it was almost impossible to simplify further.

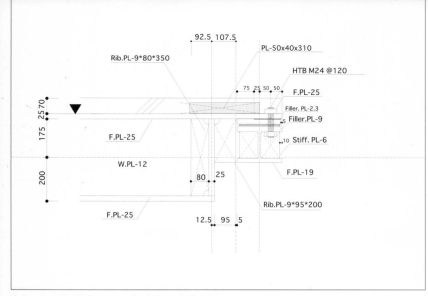

Rib.PL-9*80*350

92.5 107.5

PL-50x40x310

HTB M24 @120

75 25 50 50   F.PL-25

Filler. PL-2.3

Filler.PL-9

Stiff. PL-6

F.PL-25

W.PL-12   80   25

F.PL-19

Rib.PL-9*95*200

F.PL-25   12.5 95 5

257 0

175

200

Joint detail of honeycomb slab and ring beam

Look at the detail of the joint between the tubes and the plates (see next page). This is the floor, which is 40 cm thick. And this is the upper slab of the floor. Usually these are fixed by gusset plates and bolts, but we did not use them here; during the assembly of the first tube we found that it took so much time to reach the expected precision that we decided to make them easier to set by putting only a part of the bolt, without driving a screw, and welding them at the very end. So it´s just placed onto the ring beam. There are three reasons for this. The first is that if the slab is fixed tightly, it can cause out-of-plane deformation and distort the tubes — it has to be a kind of pin joint. The second is to avoid the tension caused by welding, which is impossible to forecast exactly in terms of where it is applied and how much; if the slab is fixed at a slightly wrong point, it will become tensed and distorted. If we just place it on the weld it without any problem. Thus we made a scheme of construction to avoid problems of dynamics and execution. The third reason is a design matter: we did them like this so that the tubes are seen to go through the slabs.

Verb: How did you manufacture these organic forms of the tubes?

Sasaki: To calculate the three-dimensional forms of the tubes and bring them into production, we sent the CAD data for the tubes to the manufacturer, Kawasaki Heavy Industries, with only the center lines of the members. They input the diameters of each member and analyzed how each piece would meet and how they should be cut three-dimensionally. There are no equal tubes, so every joint has a different angle. And each section of pipe has a groove for welding. With all of this information together, they were cut automatically by a machine working directly from the computer. It is obvious that this building could not have been constructed without these technologies, especially in the factory rather than on the construction site.

Verb: There are some parts where the structure is exposed and others where it is concealed. What is the reason behind this differentiation?

Sasaki: The original idea was that every tube would be exposed, but in the end some are covered by glass because of the need for fire compartments. Similarly, part of the slabs are made of the fire-resistant steel often used in Japan, but this is very expensive to use everywhere, so from the beginning we limited the exposed parts of the slabs to only the lower plates on the first, second, sixth and seventh floors. The upper plates do not have to be made of fire-resistant steel because they are covered by a 7-cm thick layer of concrete. These steel plates are thin, so they shrink under welding and cause a type of burr called ¨hungry horse¨. To avoid using backing on the underside of the plates, the work was done by a difficult technique called reverse-side welding. The lines still remain, but the effect is seen as the force of the material itself, which can be a form of expression in modern architecture.

Ikeda: So the welding techniques are different for the parts to be seen and not, which means the craftsmen are different, which means the labor costs are different. The average-skilled craftsmen worked on the concealed parts, welding them with backing. Similarly, the tubes for equipment are sometimes hidden inside the structure and sometimes underneath it. We had a discussion with the equipment specialist and decided everything before ordering the materials.

Sasaki: Both are problems of cost control.

Verb: What was your impression of the completed building?

Sasaki: For me, the impression of the building changed drastically three times during construction:

at the moment when the scaffolds were taken away after the completion of the structure, then when I first saw the finishings such as the glass around the tubes, and finally when the building began to be used. The first appearance with only the structure gave an impression of force. Since the building has no beams, I could judge the scale only by the tubes. When the frames of the glass were put in around the tubes, however, the scale of the structure and the finishing were so different that I confess I was disappointed, because the tubes suddenly felt like a noise in the space. But finally, when the exterior walls and the furniture were fixed and people came in, suddenly it became ¨architecture,¨ and it became very lively. I was greatly relieved.

Verb: Is the size of building appropriate for this structure?

Sasaki: The height of this building (approximately 35 m) is probably the limit for this type of structure in a country like Japan, subject to earthquakes. We did something excessive, pushed to the limit. For example, the thickest pipe is 40 mm thick (240 mm in diameter). These are solid-drawn steel pipes, and only this excessive thickness can resist earthquakes. This building is only possible today, when we have the technology that allows us to produce these thicknesses in the factory; we could only achieve 16- or 19-mm standard thicknesses before. It is a question not only of technique, but also of the ability of the steel industry and the manufacturers to realize such a difficult construction within a given budget. At the beginning of the project, I told Toyo Ito to leave half of the cost for the structure. In the end we did not use that much, and we left some parts of the structure without finishing. This building was not cheap, but after all the effort, the project finished perfectly within the expected budget.

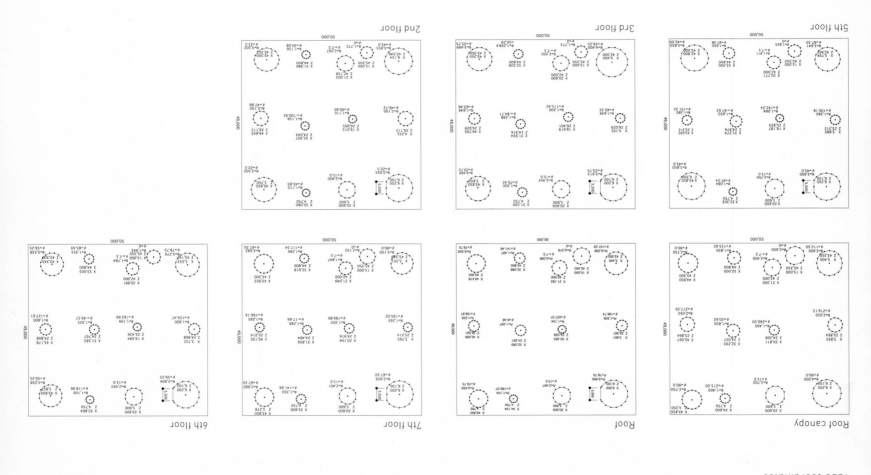

Tube coordinates

1st floor + 1st and 2nd basements

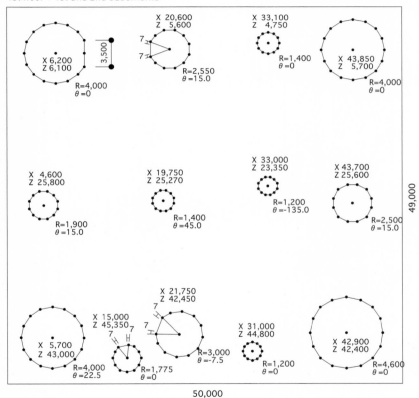

X 6,200
Z 6,100

3,500

R=4,000
θ =0

X 20,600
Z 5,600

7
7

R=2,550
θ =15.0

X 33,100
Z 4,750

R=1,400
θ =0

X 43,850
Z 5,700

R=4,000
θ =0

X 4,600
Z 25,800

R=1,900
θ =15.0

X 19,750
Z 25,270

R=1,400
θ =45.0

X 33,000
Z 23,350

R=1,200
θ =-135.0

X 43,700
Z 25,600

R=2,500
θ =15.0

X 15,000
Z 45,350

X 5,700
Z 43,000

R=4,000
θ =22.5

7
7

H

R=1,775
θ =0

X 21,750
Z 42,450

7
7

R=3,000
θ =-7.5

X 31,000
Z 44,800

R=1,200
θ =0

X 42,900
Z 42,400

R=4,600
θ =0

50,000

49,000

Overlapped plan

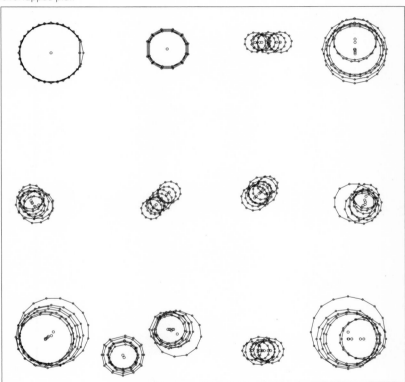

Tube assembly

Steel frame assembly work

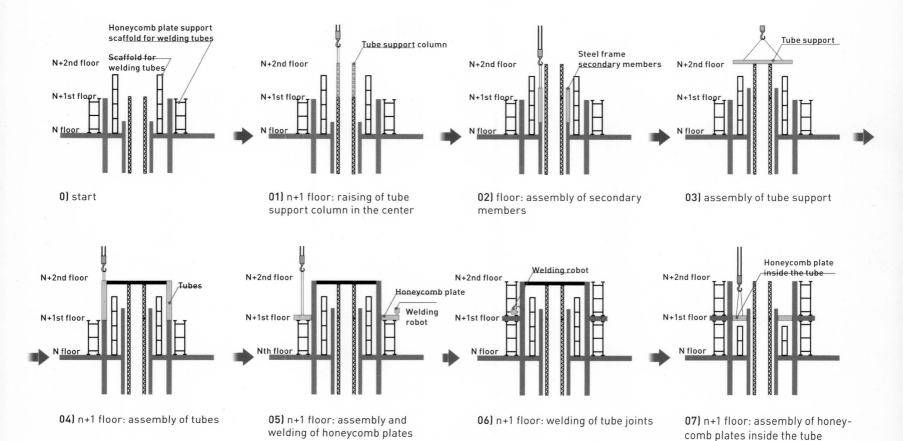

0) start

01) n+1 floor: raising of tube support column in the center

02) floor: assembly of secondary members

03) assembly of tube support

04) n+1 floor: assembly of tubes

05) n+1 floor: assembly and welding of honeycomb plates

06) n+1 floor: welding of tube joints

07) n+1 floor: assembly of honey-comb plates inside the tube

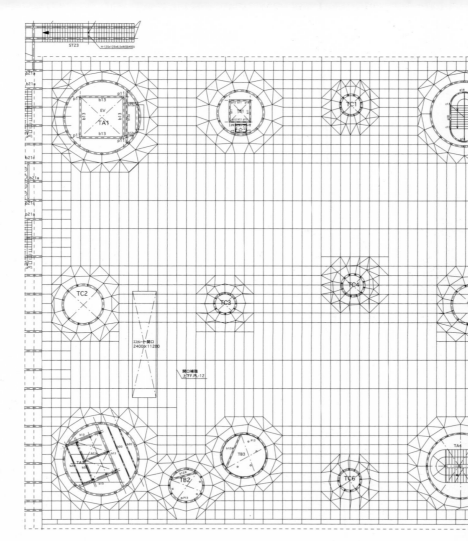

Structural plan of honeycomb plate (2nd floor)

0   10m   20m

Construction

Structure
Tube and floor plate

Working drawings of honeycomb-plate structure (2nd floor)
12 A1 drawings measuring approximately 2.5 x 2.5 meters

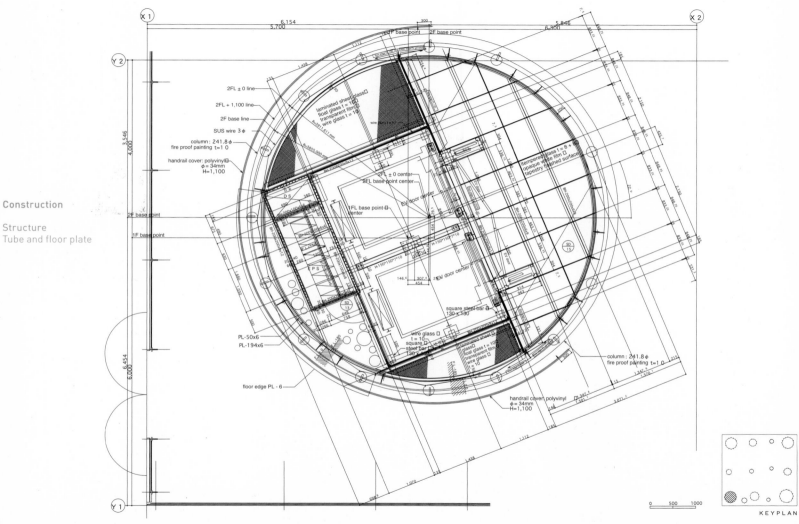

X 1   X 2

6.154   5.846
5.700   6.300

2F base point   2F base point

Y 2

2FL ± 0 line
2FL + 1,100 line   laminated sheet glass □
2F base line   float glass t = 10
SUS wire 3 φ   transparent film
                                    wire glass t = 10

column : 241.8 φ
fire proof painting t=1 0

handrail cover: polyvinyl   tempered glass t = 8 +
φ = 34mm   opaque white film
H=1,100   tapestry finished surface

2FL ± 0 center
SFL base point center

1FL base point
center   EV door center

2F base point

1F base point   H-150*150*7*10

                                    2EV door center

                                    square steel bar □
                                    130 × 130

PL-50x6   wire glass
PL-194x6   t = 10
                          square
                          steel bar □   laminated sheet
                                                     glass □
                                                     float glass t = 10
                                                     transparent film
6.454   wire glass t = 10
6.000
                                                                    column : 241.8 φ
                                                                    fire proof painting t=1 0

floor edge PL - 6

                                                     handrail cover: polyvinyl
                                                     φ = 34mm
                                                     H=1,100

Y 1

0   500   1000

KEYPLAN

Tube 1: elevator shaft, 2nd floor detail plan

Construction

Structure
Tube and floor plate

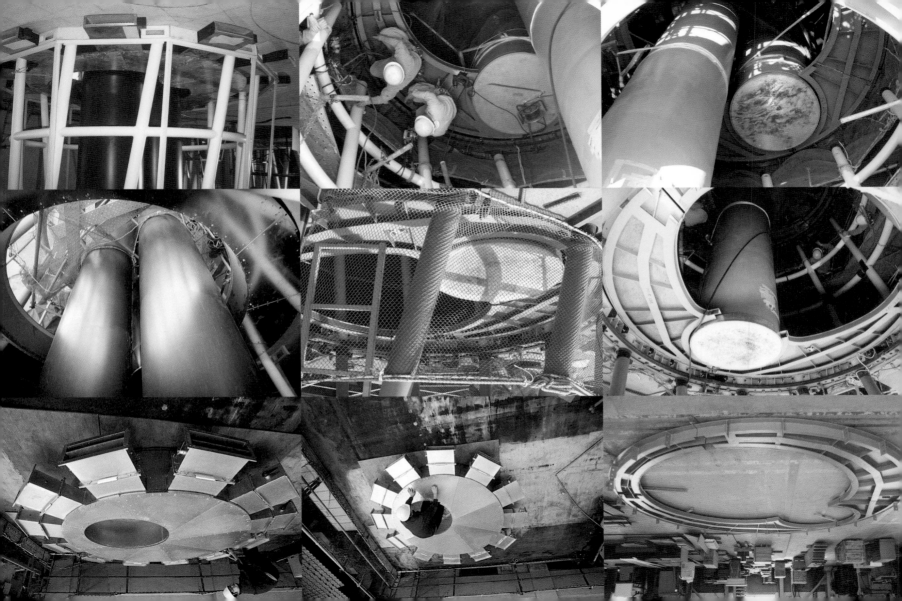

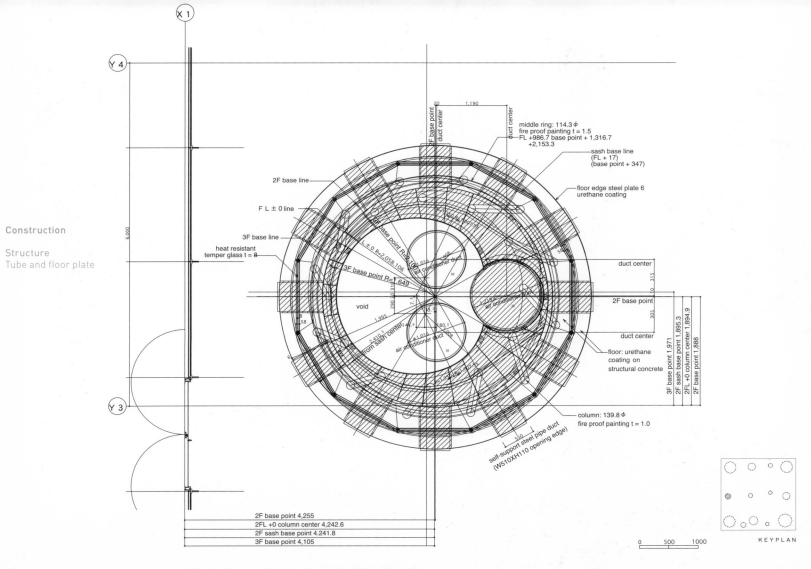

Legend (left margin):

⬜ ······
〇
〇
〇
〇

🔲 ······ **Construction**

🔴 **Structure**
Tube and floor plate

〇
〇

······ ⬜
〇
〇
〇
〇
〇
〇

Diagram labels:

X 1
Y 4
Y 3

6.000

1,190

3F base point
duct center

duct center

middle ring: 114.3 Φ
fire proof painting t = 1.5
FL +986.7 base point + 1,316.7
+2,153.3

sash base line
(FL + 17)
(base point + 347)

floor edge steel plate 6
urethane coating

2F base line

F L ± 0 line

3F base line

heat resistant
temper glass t = 8

base point R=2,058.106

air conditioner duct

3F base point R=1,649

L ± 0 R=2,058.106

void

air conditioner duct

from sash center

air conditioner duct

duct center

2F base point

duct center

floor: urethane
coating on
structural concrete

column: 139.8 Φ
fire proof painting t = 1.0

self-support steel pipe duct
(W510XH110 opening edge)

315
10
305

3F base point 1,971
2F sash base point 1,895.3
2FL +0 column center 1,894.9
2F base point 1,888

2F base point 4,255
2FL +0 column center 4,242.6
2F sash base point 4.241.8
3F base point 4,105

0   500   1000

KEYPLAN

Tube 6: air-conditioning ducts, 2nd floor detail plan

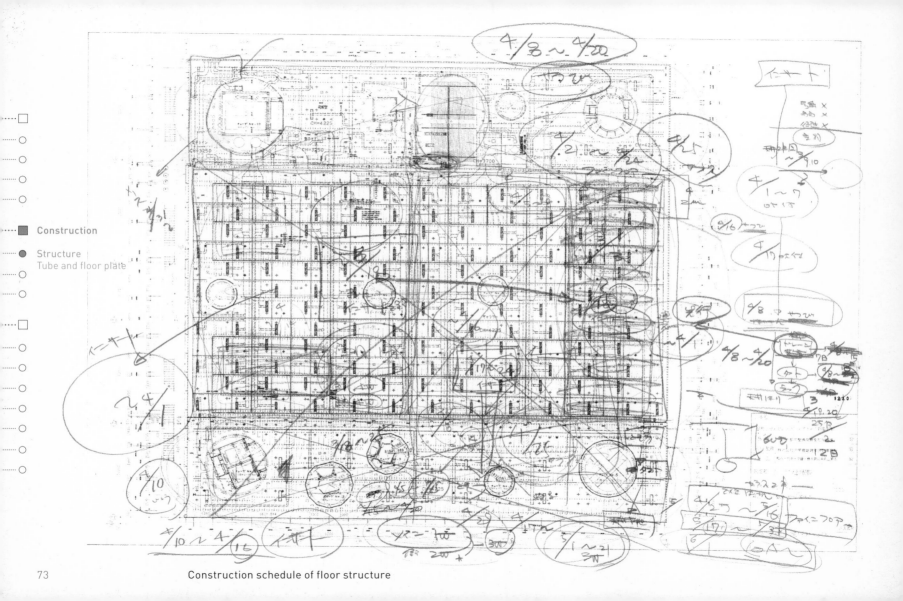

Construction

Structure
Tube and floor plate

Construction schedule of floor structure

Cross-section detail of stairwell

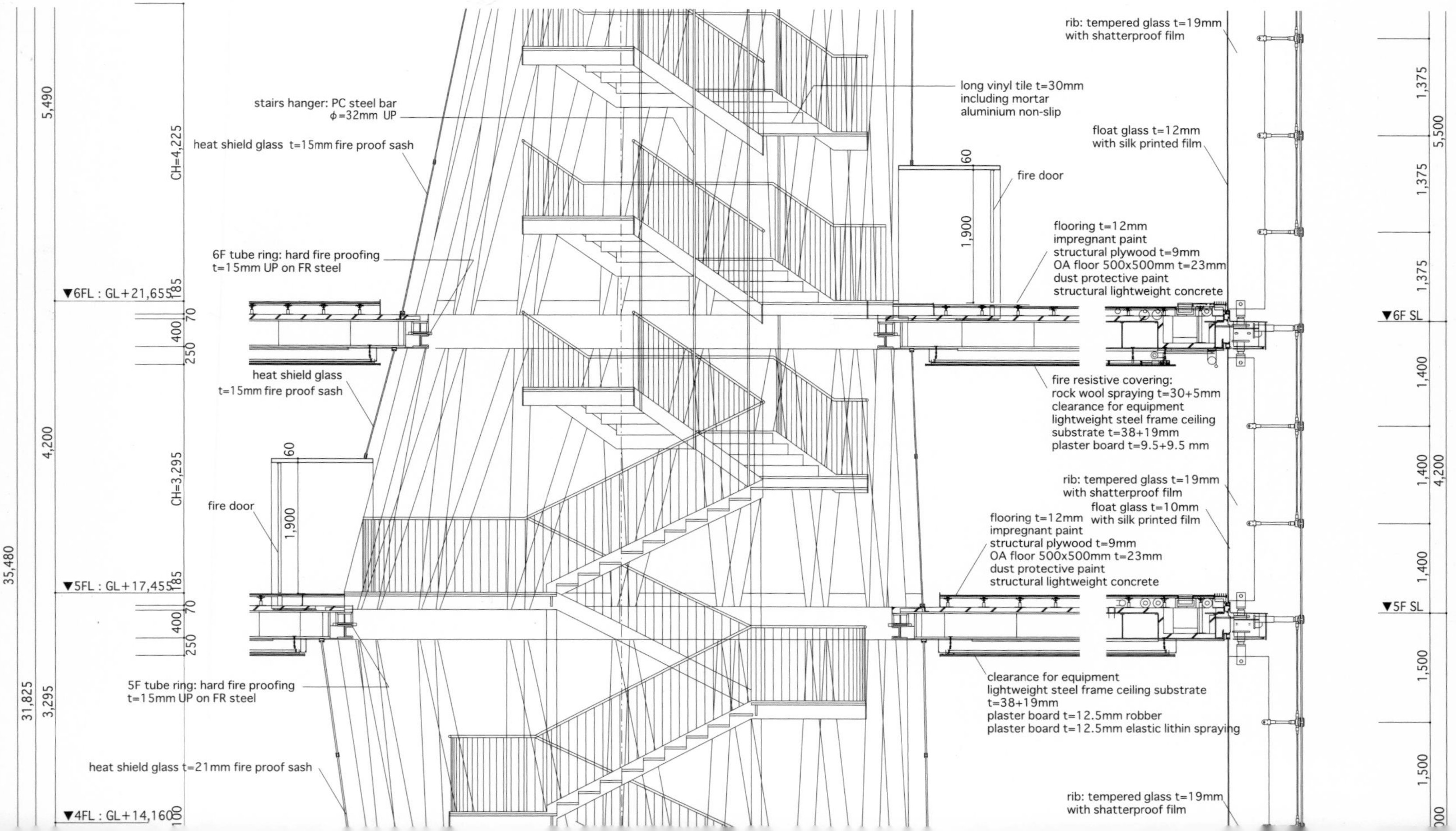

rib: tempered glass t=19mm with shatterproof film

plaster board t=12.5mm robber
plaster board t=12.5mm elastic within spraying
t=38+19mm
lightweight steel frame ceiling substrate
clearance for equipment
structural lightweight concrete
dust protective paint
OA floor 500×500mm t=23mm
structural plywood t=9mm
impregnant paint
flooring t=12mm
float glass t=10mm with silk printed film

rib: tempered glass t=19mm with shatterproof film

plaster board t=9.5+9.5 mm
substrate t=38+19mm
lightweight steel frame ceiling
clearance for equipment
fire resistive covering:
rock wool spraying t=30+5mm
structural lightweight concrete
dust protective paint
structural plywood t=9mm
impregnant paint
flooring t=12mm
float glass t=12mm with silk printed film

long vinyl tile t=30mm
including mortar
aluminium non-slip

rib: tempered glass t=19mm with shatterproof film

heat shield glass t=21 mm fire proof sash

5F tube ring: hard fire proofing
t=15mm UP on FR steel

fire door

heat shield glass
t=15mm fire proof sash

6F tube ring: hard fire proofing
t=15mm UP on FR steel

fire door

heat shield glass t=15mm fire proof sash

stairs hanger: PC steel bar
φ=32mm UP

▲4FL: GL+14,160
▲5FL: GL+17,455
▲6FL: GL+21,655

CH=3,295
CH=4,225

31,825
3,295
35,480
4,200
5,490

250 · 400 · 70 · 185

1,900 · 60

▲5F SL
▲6F SL

000
1,500
1,500
4,200
1,400
1,400
1,400
5,500
1,375
1,375
1,375

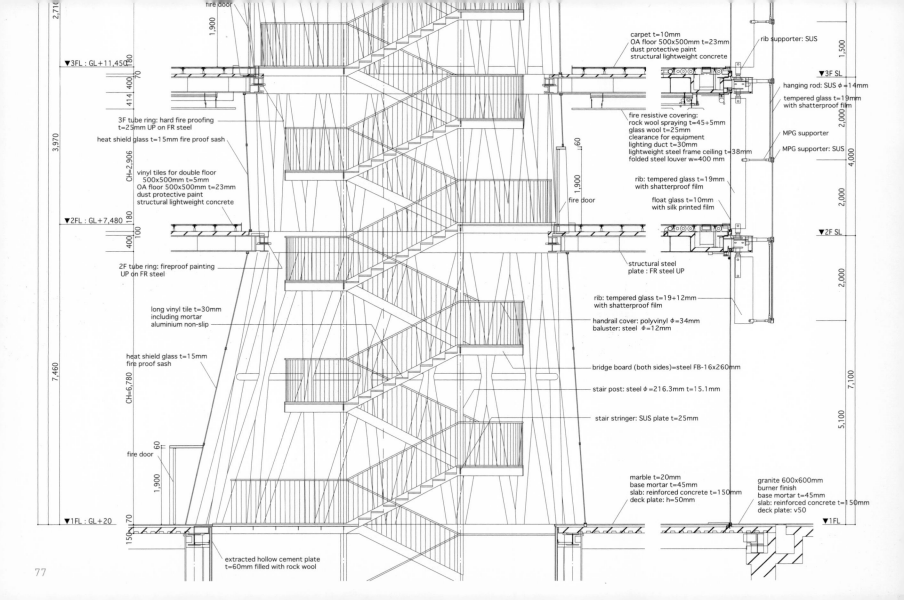

fire door

2,710

1,900

▼3FL : GL+11,450

70

400

414

3F tube ring: hard fire proofing
t=25mm UP on FR steel

heat shield glass t=15mm fire proof sash

3,970

CH=2,906

vinyl tiles for double floor
500x500mm t=5mm
OA floor 500x500mm t=23mm
dust protective paint
structural lightweight concrete

▼2FL : GL+7,480

180

100

400

2F tube ring: fireproof painting
UP on FR steel

long vinyl tile t=30mm
including mortar
aluminium non-slip

7,460

CH=6,780

heat shield glass t=15mm
fire proof sash

fire door

60

1,900

▼1FL : GL+20

150 70

extracted hollow cement plate
t=60mm filled with rock wool

carpet t=10mm
OA floor 500x500mm t=23mm
dust protective paint
structural lightweight concrete

rib supporter: SUS

1,500

▼3F SL

hanging rod: SUS φ=14mm

tempered glass t=19mm
with shatterproof film

2,000

fire resistive covering:
rock wool spraying t=45+5mm
glass wool t=25mm
clearance for equipment
lighting duct t=30mm
lightweight steel frame ceiling t=38mm
folded steel louver w=400 mm

MPG supporter

MPG supporter: SUS

4,000

rib: tempered glass t=19mm
with shatterproof film

float glass t=10mm
with silk printed film

fire door

1,900

60

2,000

▼2F SL

structural steel
plate : FR steel UP

rib: tempered glass t=19+12mm
with shatterproof film

handrail cover: polyvinyl φ=34mm
baluster: steel φ=12mm

bridge board (both sides)=steel FB-16x260mm

stair post: steel φ=216.3mm t=15.1mm

stair stringer: SUS plate t=25mm

7,100

5,100

marble t=20mm
base mortar t=45mm
slab: reinforced concrete t=150mm
deck plate: h=50mm

granite 600x600mm
burner finish
base mortar t=45mm
slab: reinforced concrete t=150mm
deck plate: v50

▼1FL

Steel-frame detail of tube and slab joint

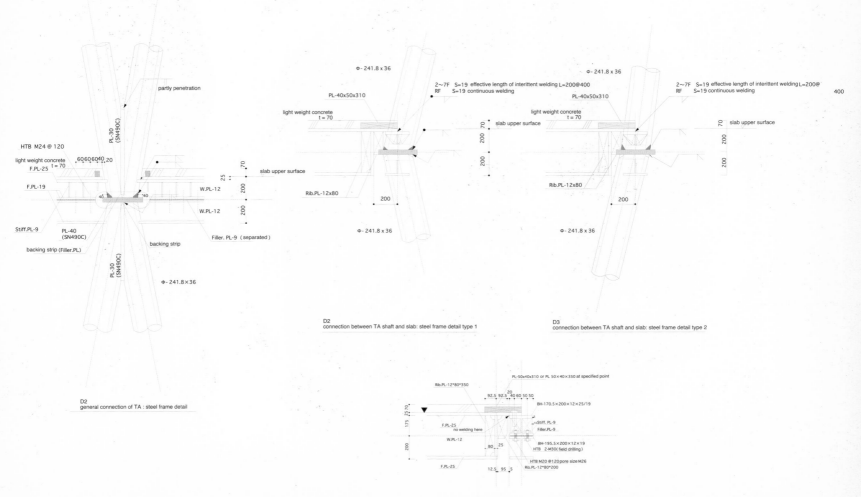

partly penetration

PL-30 (SN490C)

Φ- 241.8 x 36

PL-40x50x310

2~7F   S=19   effective length of interittent welding L=200@400
RF   S=19 continuous welding

light weight concrete
t = 70

slab upper surface

HTB M24 @ 120

light weight concrete
F.PL-25   t = 70

F.PL-19

W.PL-12

slab upper surface

W.PL-12

Rib.PL-12x80

Φ- 241.8 x 36

Stiff.PL-9

PL-40 (SN490C)

Filler. PL-9 (separated)

backing strip

backing strip (Filler.PL)

PL-30 (SN490C)

Φ- 241.8×36

D2
general connection of TA : steel frame detail

D2
connection between TA shaft and slab: steel frame detail type 1

Φ- 241.8 x 36

Φ- 241.8 x 36

light weight concrete
t = 70

slab upper surface

PL-40x50x310

2~7F   S=19   effective length of interittent welding L=200@
RF   S=19 continuous welding

400

slab upper surface

Rib.PL-12x80

Φ- 241.8 x 36

D3
connection between TA shaft and slab: steel frame detail type 2

Rib.PL-12*80*350

PL-50x40x310 or PL 50×40×350 at specified point

92.5 92.5   40 60 50 50

20

BH-170.5×200×12×25/19

F.PL-25
no welding here

Stiff. PL-9
Filler.PL-9

W.PL-12

BH-195.5×200×12×19
HTB 2-M30(field drilling)

F.PL-25

HTB M20 @120 pore size M26
Rib.PL-12*80*200

connection between honeycob slab of TA shaft and ring beam

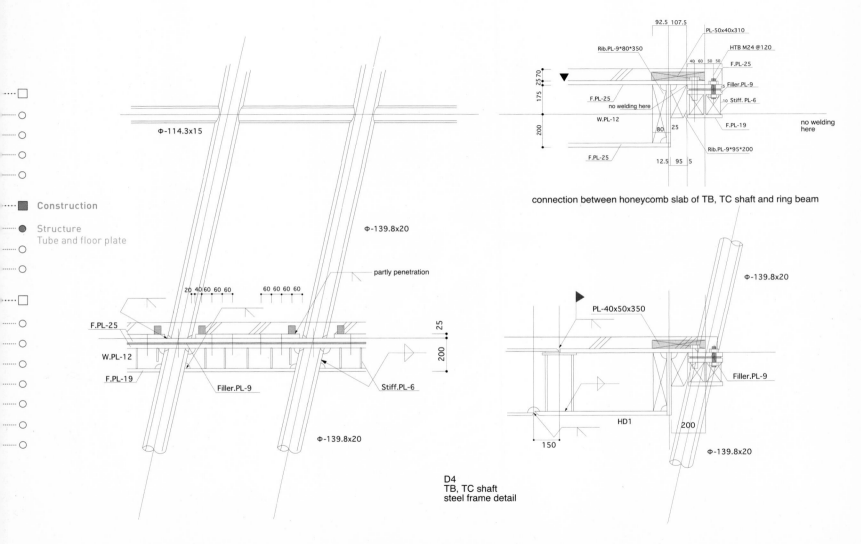

Construction

Structure
Tube and floor plate

Φ-114.3x15

Φ-139.8x20

partly penetration

20 40 60 60 60   60 60 60 60

F.PL-25

W.PL-12

F.PL-19

Filler.PL-9

Stiff.PL-6

25

200

Φ-139.8x20

92.5 107.5

PL-50x40x310

Rib.PL-9*80*350

HTB M24 @120

40 60 50 50

F.PL-25

25 70

175

Filler.PL-9

F.PL-25

no welding here

Stiff. PL-6

200

W.PL-12

no welding here

F.PL-19

80   25

F.PL-25

Rib.PL-9*95*200

12.5   95   5

connection between honeycomb slab of TB, TC shaft and ring beam

Φ-139.8x20

PL-40x50x350

Filler.PL-9

HD1

200

150

Φ-139.8x20

D4
TB, TC shaft
steel frame detail

Detail section of double-glass skin

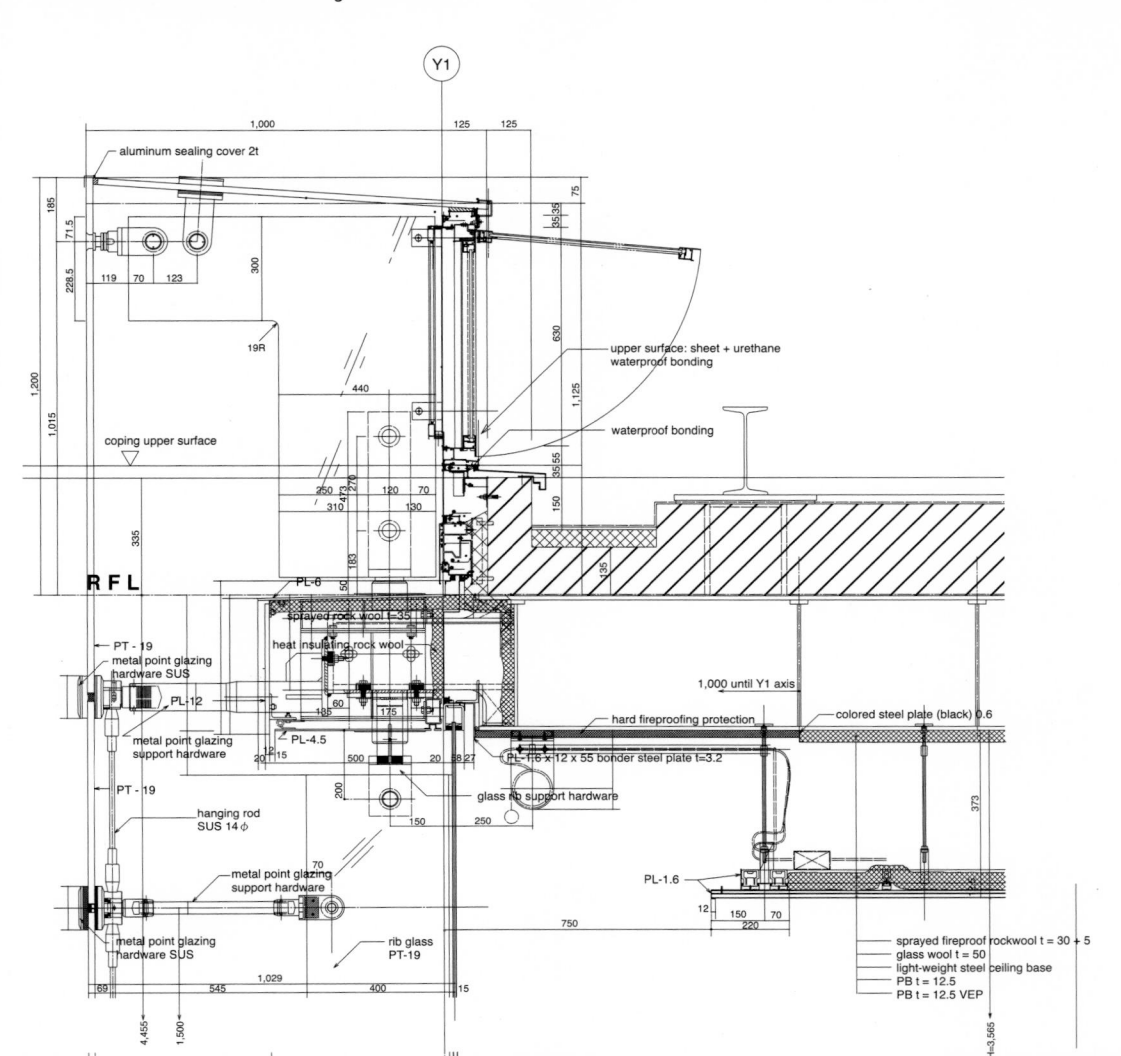

Y1

aluminum sealing cover 2t

upper surface: sheet + urethane
waterproof bonding

waterproof bonding

coping upper surface

RFL

PT - 19

metal point glazing
hardware SUS

PL-12

metal point glazing
support hardware

PT - 19

hanging rod
SUS 14 φ

metal point glazing
support hardware

metal point glazing
hardware SUS

rib glass
PT-19

sprayed rock wool t=35

heat insulating rock wool

PL-6

PL-4.5

glass rib support hardware

PL-116 x 12 x 55 bonder steel plate t=3.2

hard fireproofing protection

colored steel plate (black) 0.6

1,000 until Y1 axis

PL-1.6

sprayed fireproof rockwool t = 30 + 5
glass wool t = 50
light-weight steel ceiling base
PB t = 12.5
PB t = 12.5 VEP

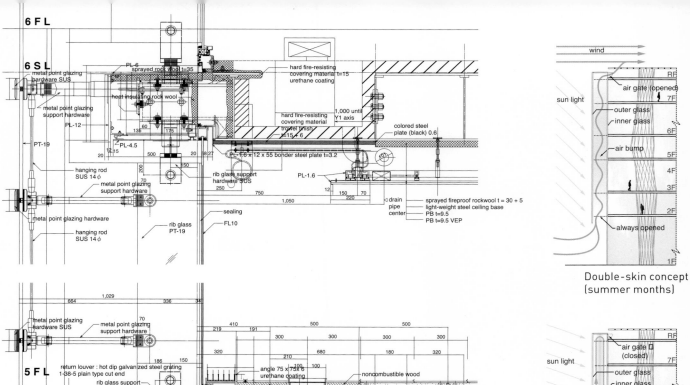

6 F L

6 S L

metal point glazing
hardware SUS

metal point glazing
support hardware

PL-6
sprayed rock wool t=35

heat insulating rock wool

PL-12

PL-4.5

PT-19

hanging rod
SUS 14 φ

metal point glazing
support hardware

metal point glazing hardware

hanging rod
SUS 14 φ

60

135 175

12 15

20

500

20 38 27

200

150

70

250

sealing

rib glass
PT-19

FL10

hard fire-resisting
covering material t=15
urethane coating

1,000 until
Y1 axis

hard fire-resisting
covering material
trowel finish
t=15 × 6

PL-1.6 × 12 × 55 bonder steel plate t=3.2

rib glass support
hardware SUS

PL-1.6

750

1,050

12

150 70

220

colored steel
plate (black) 0.6

drain
pipe
center

sprayed fireproof rockwool t = 30 + 5
light-weight steel ceiling base
PB t=9.5
PB t=9.5 VEP

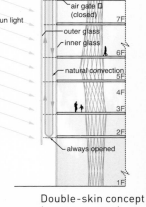

wind

sun light

RF
air gate (opened)
7F
outer glass
inner glass
6F
air bump
5F
4F
3F
2F
always opened
1F

**Double-skin concept
(summer months)**

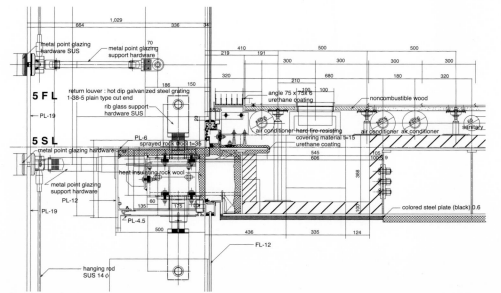

metal point glazing
hardware SUS

metal point glazing
support hardware

664 1,029 336 34

70

219 410 191

320

186 150

300 300 300 300

210

680 180 320

5 F L

return louver : hot dip galvanized steel grating
1-38-5 plain type cut end

rib glass support
hardware SUS

PL-19

PL-6
sprayed rock wool t=35

5 S L

metal point glazing hardware

heat insulating rock wool

metal point glazing
support hardware

PL-12

PL-4.5

PL-19

135 175

60

500

angle 75 × 75 × 6
urethane coating

air conditioner hard fire-resisting
covering material t=15
urethane coating

noncombustible wood

air conditioner air conditioner

545
606

388

sanitary

colored steel plate (black) 0.6

436 335 124

FL-12

hanging rod
SUS 14 φ

sun light

RF
air gate □
(closed)
7F
outer glass
inner glass
6F
natural convection
5F
4F
3F
2F
always opened
1F

**Double-skin concept
(winter months)**

Detail of tube sash

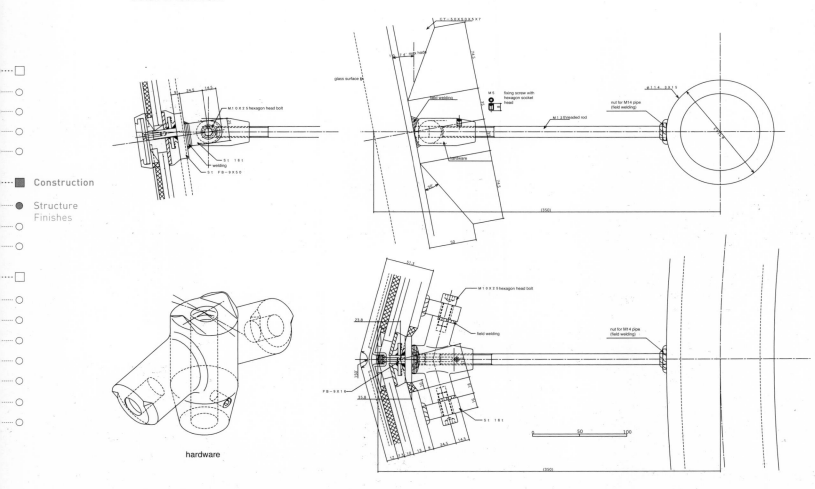

hardware

Geometry of tube glass (1)
There are 1,548 different shapes of panels in 3 different types of glass
according to fire-prevention requirements on each floor.

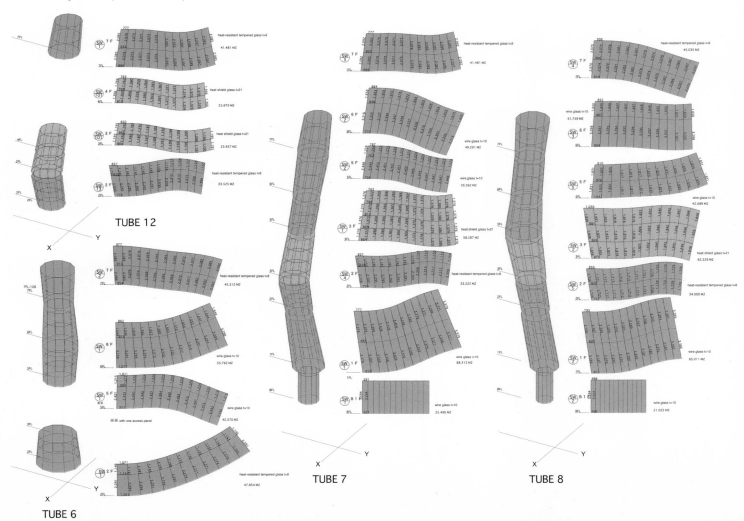

TUBE 12

TUBE 6

TUBE 7

TUBE 8

Geometry of tube glass (2)

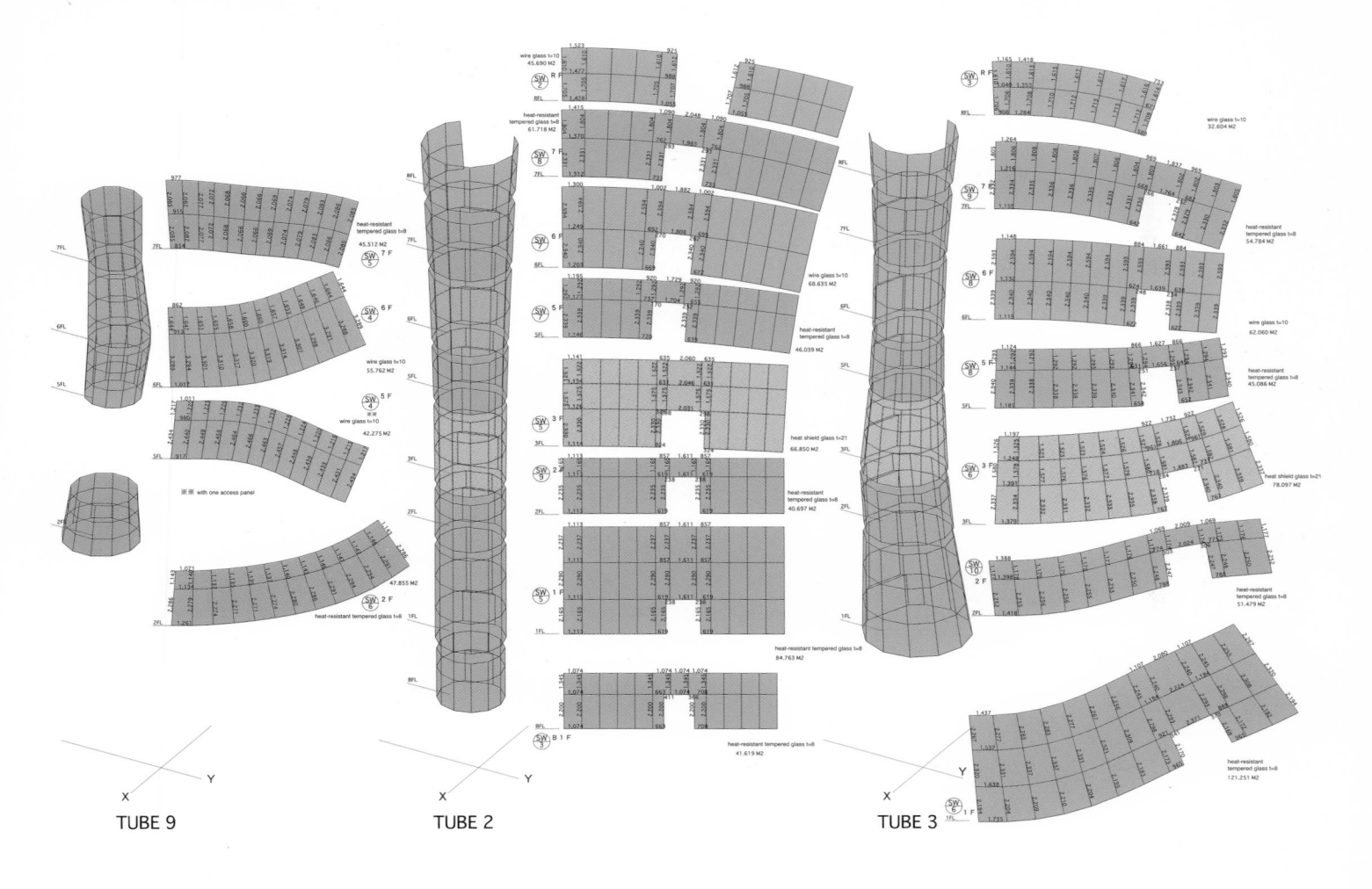

TUBE 9

TUBE 2

TUBE 3

Geometry of tube glass (3)

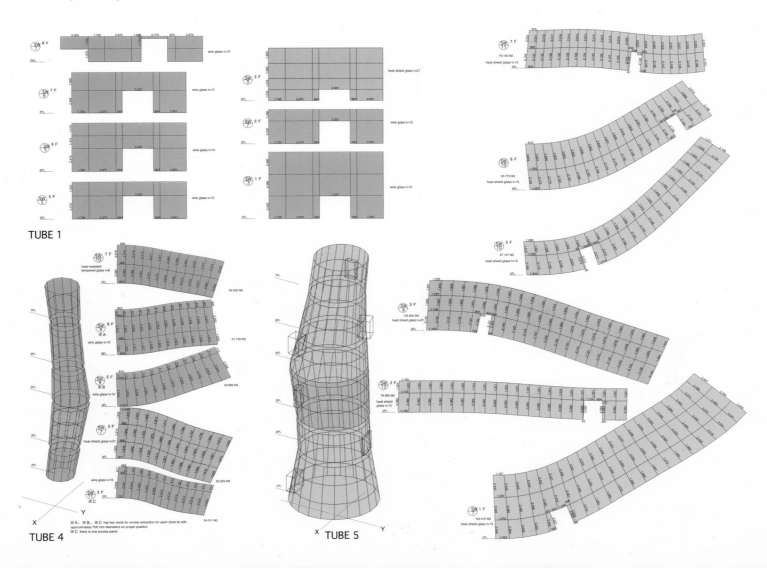

TUBE 1

TUBE 4

※A, ※B, ※C has two ducts for smoke extraction for each (total 6) with approximately 700 mm diameters on proper position
※C there is one access panel

TUBE 5

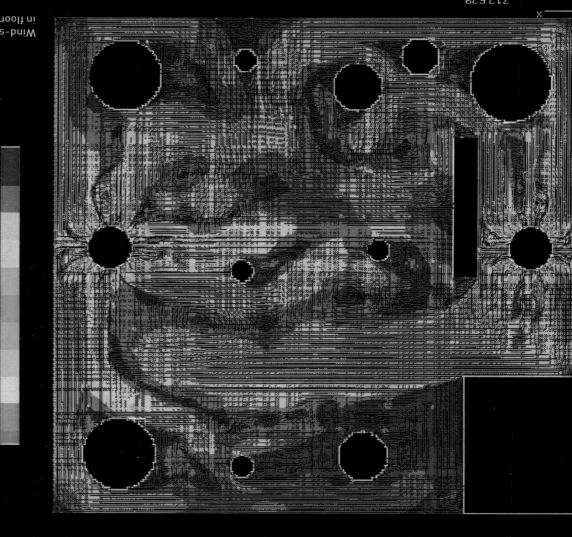

Wind-speed distribution
in floor slab

VECT

0

9.47688

712.629

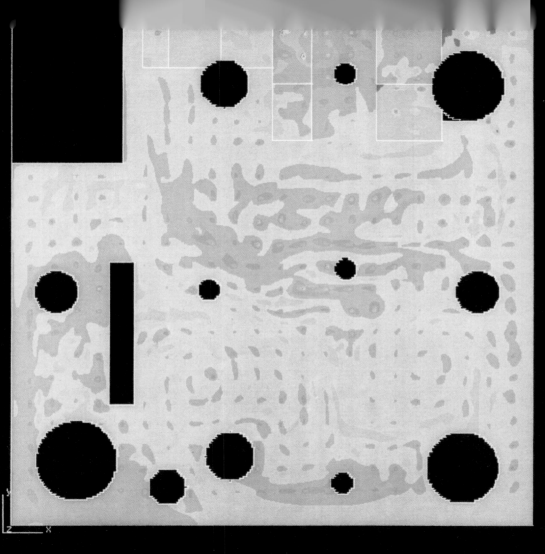

Temperature distribution
at 1.1 m above floor surface

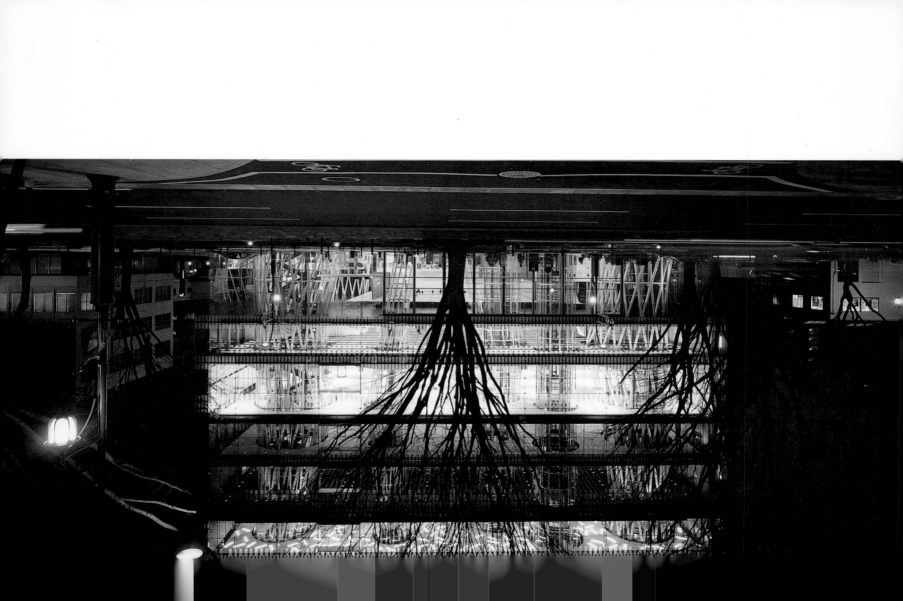

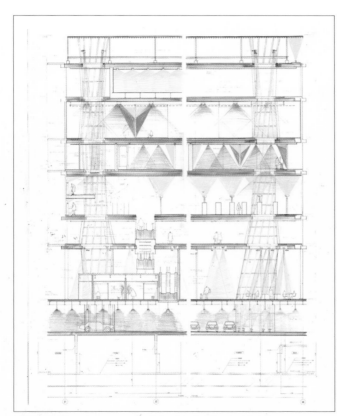

Lighting planning concept. Drawing by Kaoru Mende

Lighting

Verb: In the Sendai Mediatheque each floor has a different color of light. Was this the original lighting concept?

Kaoru Mende: The basic lighting concept in the Sendai Mediatheque is that white light accumulates in the underground floors and flows up through the building at night. White-blue fluorescent lamps are used in the basement, and inside the tubes we use mercury lamps that have high color temperature in blue. Warmer colors are used in the upper floors, against which the white-blue light can be seen rising up from the basement. In fact however, light is reflected on the floors and ceilings, so its color changes depending on the finishes of each level. This is what produces the effect of different colored lights stacked up on top of each other. The original concept of white lights going through warm lights became a bit more complicated in the end.

Verb: But this stacking of colors reveals the general concept of the architecture — that of the tubes connecting layers of different programs.

Kaoru Mende: When I first saw a sketch of the building by Toyo Ito I did not imagine such a chaotic diversity. But during the design process Toyo Ito said regarding the different programs that the building was 'like a convenience store of media'. Then I realized that each floor could have different lighting characteristics according to each function, and that this variation could be seen like the different layers of a city.

Verb: Could you describe the lighting control systems?

Kaoru Mende: Each floor has a very precise lighting control system that adapts it to the gradual change of brightness outside. This was not easy in the case of the fluorescent lamps on 7th floor, where we had to program two separate control levels for the lighting voltage in different areas. For the library on the 3rd floor we had planned a super-ambient light that would rebound from the upper side of every shelf, but controlling this system became too difficult as the shelves were not placed in regular, parallel lines.

Verb: Finally you used lamps suspended from the ceiling, which I heard people here call UFOs... I think that the lighting of this building is probably at its best when it is getting dark outside.

Kaoru Mende: This is the specific lighting characteristic of glass buildings. The luminosity of interior and exterior space — the darker and brighter side of the building — turns over at this point. And I think it is very interesting to have two points of view, from the inside and from the outside.

Basic concept - color temperature

Our task here was to materialize the architectural concept of the Mediatheque through its lighting design, and to create comfortable environments suitable to each of the floors, with their different functions and ceiling heights. At the same time, we were in charge of verifying all aspects related to the lighting maintenance and its running costs suited to a public facility of this kind. At the construction design stage in 1997, we set two basic color temperatures: 3500 K for the floors and 5000 K for the tubes. The light on each floor would be different depending on the specific design and fixture of the light source, but they would all be crossed by the bright lines of the tubes that run through the building.

2F: In the 50 x 50 meter plan, the difference of the illuminance between the window side and the center could be 100 to 1, so the theme was to average it by using the natural sunlight source of the tubes and by partially reducing that of the façades. The artificial lighting system, on the other hand, is divided into small circuits which are programmed under 4 levels of intensities. The average of horizontal illuminance is set at 750 lux.

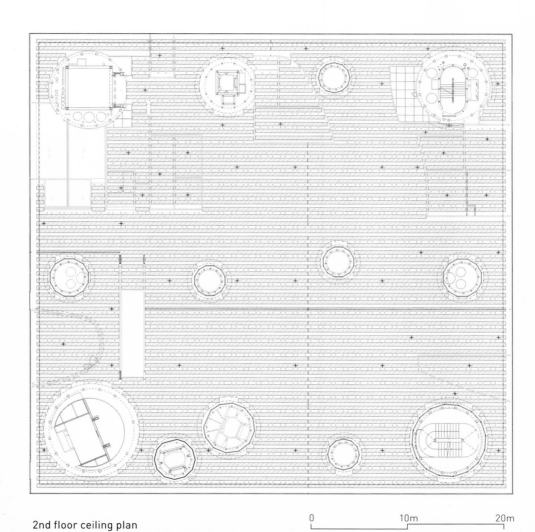

2nd floor ceiling plan

0   10m   20m

3F: The ceiling height here is 5.2 meters, so we designed a special lighting fixture with a metal halide lamp that produces 'super-ambient' lighting. The illuminance is affected by the ceiling's luminous efficiency, reflectance and brilliance, so we also did a lot of research on the finishes. The average horizontal illuminance on the floor is 500 lux.

Construction

Lighting

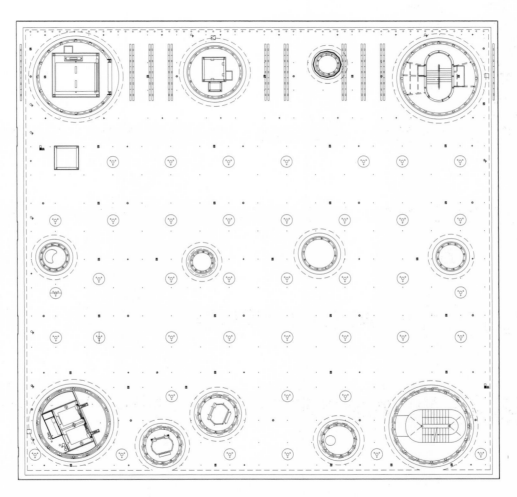

4th floor ceiling plan

0   10m   20m

7F: The typical parallel placement of fluorescent lights in office spaces tends to create shadows in its orthogonal direction. The layout of the Mediatheque's 7th floor is based on curving walls and movable furniture, so we arranged the fluorescent tubes accordingly in a totally random layout that erases any sense of direction. The lighting vectors are shuffled and eliminate shadows in any direction.

Construction

Lighting

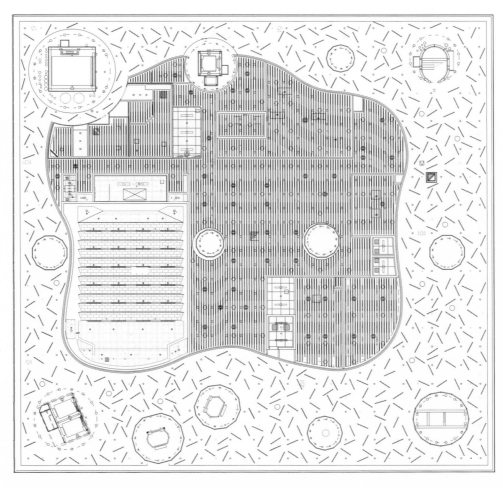

7th floor ceiling plan

0   10m   20m

Tubes: Independently of the lighting of each floor, mercury lamps in a clair-de-lune color are used in all of the tubes. At night, the tubes are emphasized so as to reveal the structure more clearly. The 13 tubes have different shapes and diameters, and maintenance work inside is often difficult. After initial discussions on the possible use of fiber-optic cable lamps, LED or long-lasting fluorescent lights, we adopted the most simple solution of alloy lights that run throughout the entire length of the tube's interior.

Sunlight tracking system: Two of the tubes located in the center of the floor plan are equipped with a sunlight tracking system on the top that brings natural light into the building. Besides reducing energy costs, the presence of natural light in the center of the 50 x 50 meter floor is also a source of great comfort. The system performance is 100,000 lumens, and is supposed to distribute 3,000 lumens for each floor. Sunlight also illuminates the interior of the tubes.

After the project by Toyo Ito and Associates was selected in the open competition held by the city of Sendai, the Sendai Mediatheque Project Team was set up to seek a concrete definition of the activities that were to take place in this novel public facility. The guidelines approved by this team were stated in the following principles:

1. **The Sendai Mediatheque flexibly serves the needs of people by supplying the latest knowledge and culture.**
2. **The Sendai Mediatheque maximizes networking potentials through nodes rather than terminals.**
3. **The Sendai Mediatheque serves all people including the disabled, users, providers, and people of different languages and cultures, by allowing unobstructed access to the premises and its programs / through freeing them of all barriers.**

Verb: How was this committee set up?
Akira Suzuki: Our meetings started during the design phase following the competition, with the goal of producing concepts for the building activities, and not only for the architectural program. Our task was to define what the Sendai Mediatheque would be, and explain it to the citizens.
Initially, the members of this committee were: Minoru Kanno, professor of Tohoku University and one of the jurors in the design competition; the critic Koji Taki; Toshie Suzuki, an advisor of the continuing education department of the Ministry of Education; Eishi Katsura, professor of library science; Yasuaki Onoda, a lecturer of Tohoku University, and Emiko Okuyama, head of the continuing education department of the city of Sendai who subsequently became the director of the Sendai Mediatheque. Although the architectural design had already begun, our work addressed the original concept and organization of the Mediatheque. What we discussed there would have to be reflected in the subsequent development of the design.
But somehow, our ultimate conclusion was the extreme realization that we had to 'avoid fixing the program'.

During our discussions, Eishi Katsura stated a basic direction to follow, saying that this facility had to serve as a community center for the citizens in this area. We studied a lot about research facilities for contemporary art and information technologies, but the original base for this project had to be that of a community center and city library. Thus, instead of trying to turn it into an experimental facility, the mediatheque had to be first of all a place servicing the citizens, like a library where one can read or borrow books. For that, we would share the information with other facilities.

There are also very important consequences deriving from the 'not terminals but nodes' guideline. When we try to create a new facility, we tend to think of it as a 'center'. Here instead we wanted it to be a 'hub', meaning that people come here and then go somewhere else. The only thing we do is to set up a network.

Verb: What is the role of the workshops?

Akira Suzuki: They are one of the basic activities in the Mediatheque, conceived as an open-ended activity rather than one leading to a conclusion or a goal. People working in the Mediatheque make plans and execute them, searching for new ways to use this facility. For example, we did a workshop on letterpress printing, a method which is at the very base of all printed media, and has various limits or rules that we don't recognize in digital printing. This is a culture in itself. And we keep this workshop moving, as a single case in Japan.

Verb: How did the tactile model originate?

Akira Suzuki: The Mediatheque is also an information center for the vision- or hearing-impaired, so we studied how to provide barrier-free services. Interviews with vision-impaired people revealed that the typical tactile map on the wall is very expensive and that very few people use it. One day, Toyo Ito did a public presentation of the project using both drawings and models. A teacher for the blind touched and grasped a big model at 1/50 scale, and said 'I understand. This building is very different from the usual building'. We were inspired by this experience and made the tactile model. This is a model of the floor plan with Braille inscriptions put on the desk, and when you touch it, it speaks to you and guides you through the plan. Everybody uses it.

Construction

Program

Different brochures: general guide, smt access,
library guide, English guide and wheelchair access

Verb: What is the signage planning concept?

Akira Suzuki: During the process of discussion about signage we decided to visit Tokyo Disneyland. There we saw the sweepers had maps and guided the visitors. This inspired the wearable sign. The concept is quickness — when visitors ask the staff for directions, they can guide them immediately. We prepared various types of map, for instance one for wheelchair access. We didn't make a map for all needs, but different maps for various requirements. This is a part of signage planning. This map was also made following interviews with wheelchair users.

Of course, there were many unexpected issues that came up after the opening, and we constantly have to update the information. We do these activities not in response to a request from the city of Sendai, but as volunteer work. As we said, this facility is always under construction, and we will continue these activities to keep the Mediatheque changing in the future.

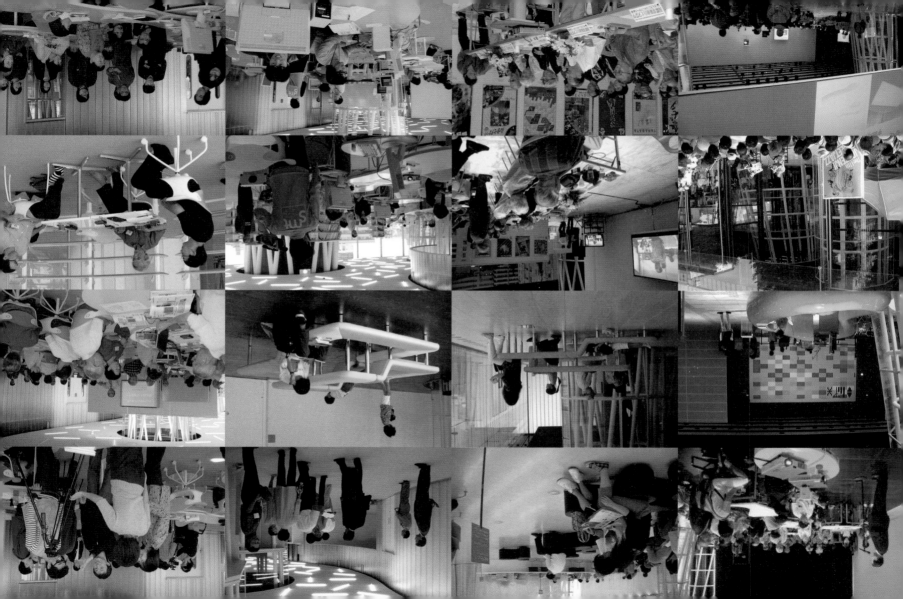

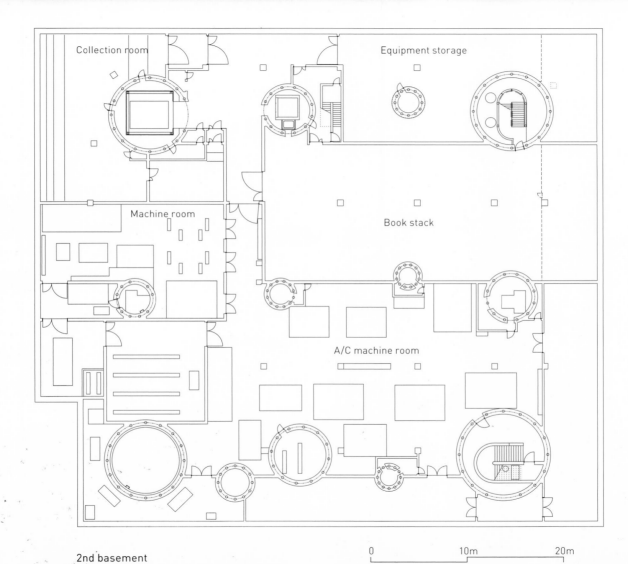

Collection room

Equipment storage

Machine room

Book stack

A/C machine room

Use

Evolution
Building tour

2nd basement

0   10m   20m

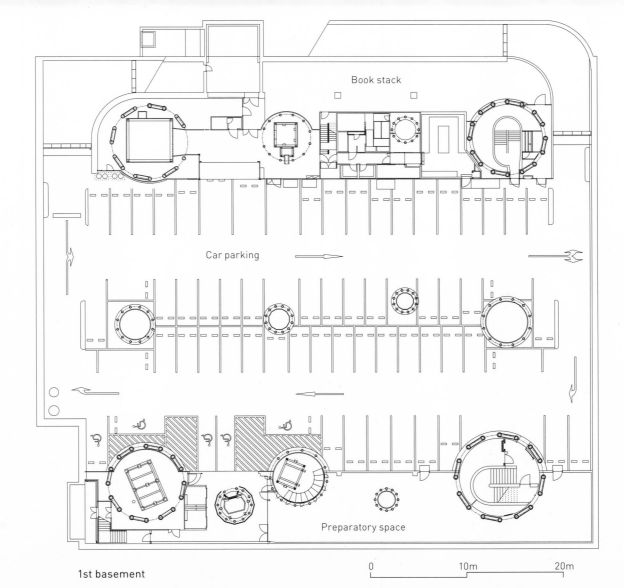

Book stack

Car parking

Preparatory space

Use

Evolution
Building tour

1st basement

0   10m   20m

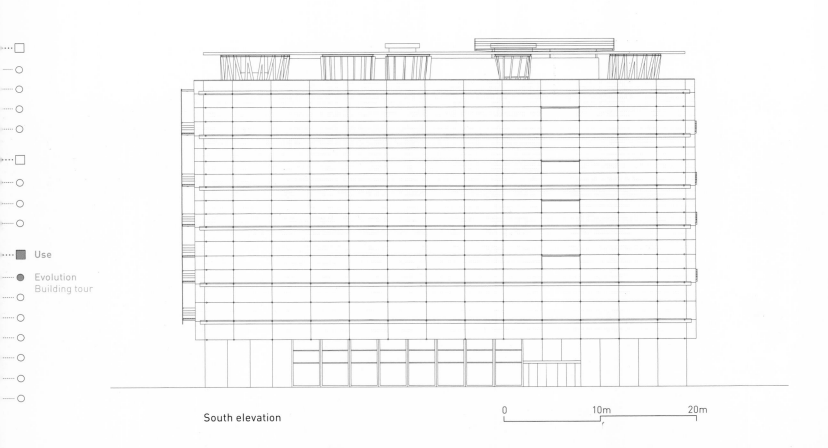

South elevation

0   10m   20m

Use

Evolution
Building tour

East elevation

0   10m   20m

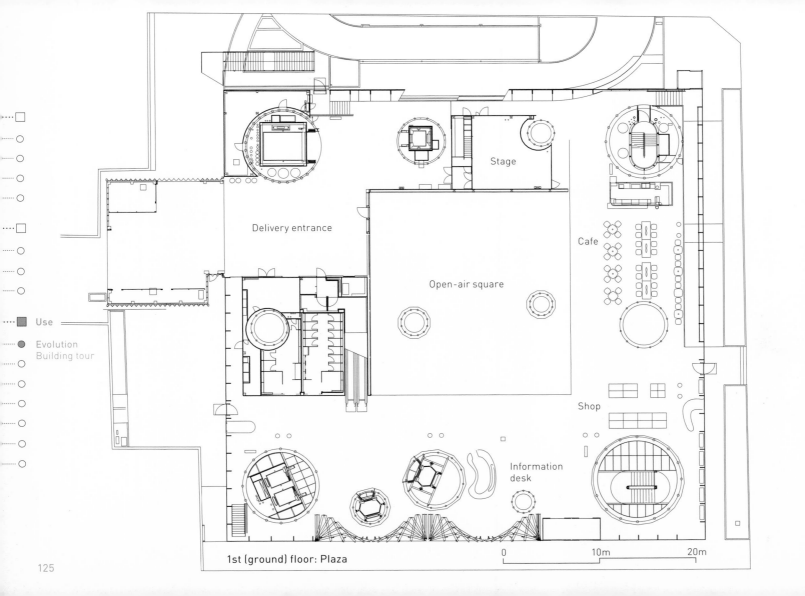

Use

Evolution
Building tour

Delivery entrance

Stage

Cafe

Open-air square

Shop

Information
desk

1st (ground) floor: Plaza

0   10m   20m

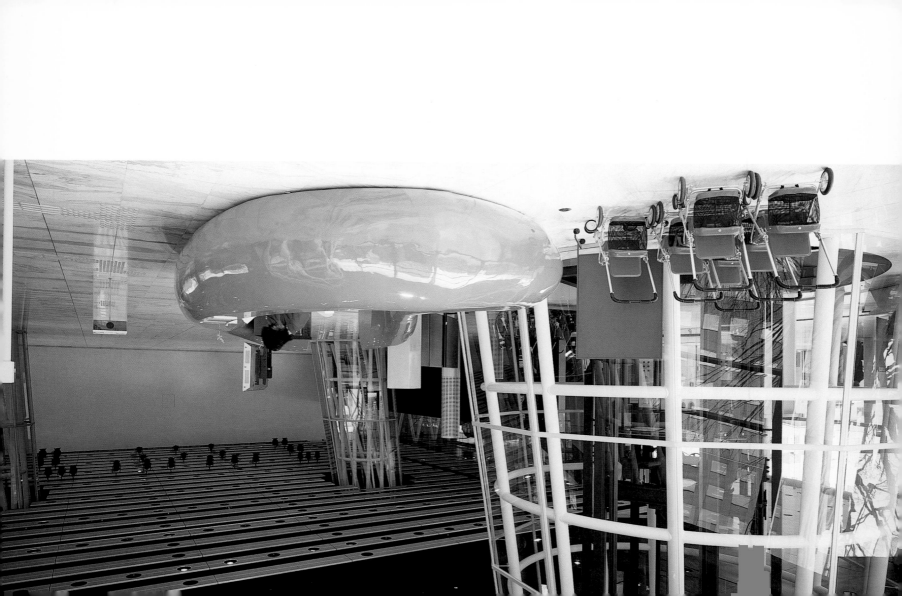

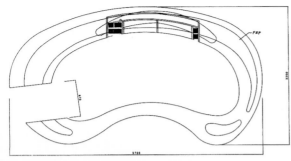

Information counter designed by Karim Rashid

Evolution
Interview with Emiko Okuyama, director of the Sendai Mediatheque, and Yasuaki Onoda,
assistant professor of Tohoku University, Sendai

Verb: How did the Mediatheque project begin?

Yasuaki Onoda: It began in 1994. At that time, the city of Sendai was growing rapidly, and needed new community facilities to keep up with this growth. The city gallery was temporarily located in a rented space inside a private department store, with a very short lease. Sendai had no museum, and the library was old and its use required immediate renovation. And on Jozenji Street, which is one of the most important and beautiful avenues in the city, there was this plot occupied by a pachinko parlor and a switchyard for the buses, therefore destroying the neighborhood. So it was decided to turn this site into a new public institution, which would include a gallery, a library, an audiovisual media center, and a barrier-free information center for senior, handicapped and foreign people. The city of Sendai decided to hold an open competition to select the architect, and asked our Sugano studio in Tohoku University to help them draw an entry application procedure and the guidelines for the competition.

We proposed to add two more conceptual functions (information and art) and made a diagram including workshop activities. We also agreed to ask Arata Isozaki to preside over the competition jury. He had already agreed to be on the jury of the Yokohama International Terminal competition that was held almost at the same time, and initially he rejected our request. But we did a presentation explaining our ideas, and finally he accepted. It was his suggestion to name this building a 'mediatheque'. This was a concept which already existed in France, but not yet in Japan. It was hard to explain it to the administration, but everybody was interested in the newness of this name.

Emiko Okuyama: Mr. Isozaki thought that we needed the spirit of the name of the institution. I also think that if we had called it something like 'cultural information center' we wouldn't have achieved the same results.

Verb: Do you think that the Mediatheque will be a specific type of community facility in the future?

Emiko Okuyama: Yes, I hope so. That's why we named it 'Sendai' Mediatheque. Mr. Ito also thought of it as a beginning or a prototype.

Verb: How did you decide on the program? Given that one of its distinctive features is the workshop, did you have the idea of making the program evolve rather than setting up fixed facilities?

Emiko Okuyama: The idea of the workshops was not part of the initial plans of the city administration. But Mr. Onoda gave us this idea as a way to bring together the four basic functions: gallery, library, audiovisual media center and barrier-free information center. I would say that there are three main pillars on which the Sendai Mediatheque was founded: the name 'Mediatheque' from Mr. Isozaki, the idea of workshop from Mr. Onoda, and the actual building from Mr. Ito.

Yasuaki Onoda: It was very difficult to decide on a fixed program. Finally this process was left open and instead we tried to make something like a meta-decision.

Use

Evolution

Verb: What kinds of workshops have been held up to now?

Emiko Okuyama: We have done various sorts of workshops, like on letterpress or blueprint photographs of the sun. There are different levels of workshop, but in our opinion they have not yet caught up with the ideal type of workshop, like having our staff take part in a workshop aimed at planning future workshops.

Verb: I heard that in the letterpress workshop you brought in not only the machinery, but also hired an artisan.

Emiko Okuyama: A retired artisan comes here to teach us. We would like to inherit part of his skill, even a small portion of it. It is a very difficult and slow technique, but it is very interesting for its strong physical limits.

Yasuaki Onoda: For us this is in a way a metaphor of media. When an artisan sets a machine in motion, it makes a big noise, and everybody around it is impressed and wonders what it will produce. The letterpress machine exists as a center of attention. We are trying to exchange knowledge of a kind of tacit intellect that is usually shared unconsciously. The Mediatheque can be a platform for this type of experience.

Verb: The library here also exists within physical limits. We can look for information on the Internet, but here we are in a physical space in which we find information in the materiality of the books.

Emiko Okuyama: Books are ideas and emotions made into objects. We would miss this if the Sendai Media-theque dealt only with electronic media.

Verb: How do you decide on the workshop themes?

Yasuaki Onoda: We don't, we simply rent our facilities to conduct workshops that are conceived outside. The Mediatheque staff give advice, and we offer the technical equipment in our spaces to support these activities. Every workshop is recorded and kept in the library archives, both digitally and in printed form. At the same time, we make efforts to develop the literacy of people in new digital media.

Use

Evolution

Study of the use of public open space / open square
This is the first building in Japan which contains a public open space

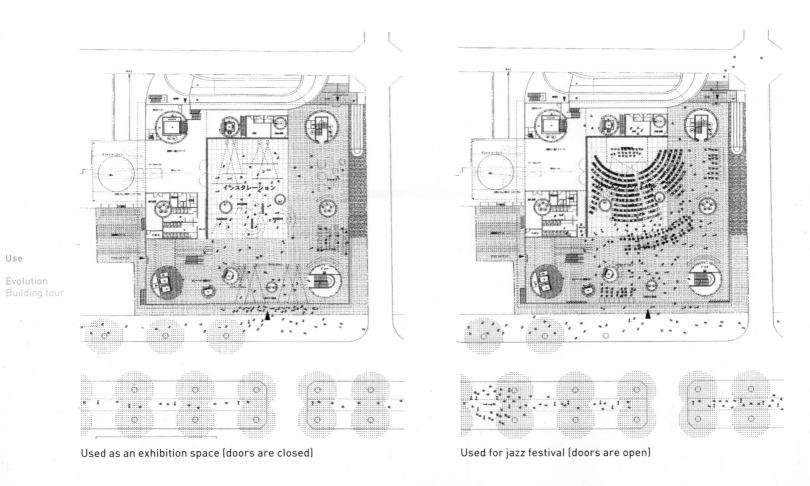

Use

Evolution
Building tour

Used as an exhibition space (doors are closed)

Used for jazz festival (doors are open)

Verb: One of the basic ideas of the Sendai Mediatheque is to 'leave the possibilities for future change open'. What does this possibility mean?

Yasuaki Onoda: Physically, the limits of each space are not strictly defined. They work as both room space and circulation space, as a sort of buffer zone between functions. Spaces have names, but they appear as a succession of activities. We were imagining an open spatial organization analogous to the LINUX operational system.

Emiko Okuyama: There are very few walls in the Mediatheque. Walls usually provide a clear definition of what happens inside rooms, but Mr. Onoda suggested that here we would have furniture instead of walls, and funiture can be moved. Rooms are generally wide and open, but we can perceive different degrees of activity within them. There are also very few meeting rooms, as meetings are usually conducted within larger open spaces.

Verb: Isn't it too noisy then?

Yasuaki Onoda: The interesting thing is that people have to be aware of and negotiate with other users. We can learn a lot of things while we use the Mediatheque. It not only provides services to the community, but it is also a place where the sense of community comes into being.

Verb: How do you think people have reacted to the Mediatheque?

Emiko Okuyama: Each person accepts it and uses it in his or her individual way. People are not necessarily conscious of the difference between this building and other public facilities, I think they simply come here naturally. Everybody seems to accept and enjoy the spaces and the activities. People in the neighborhood come here to take a walk, and sometimes even to take a nap...

Use

Evolution

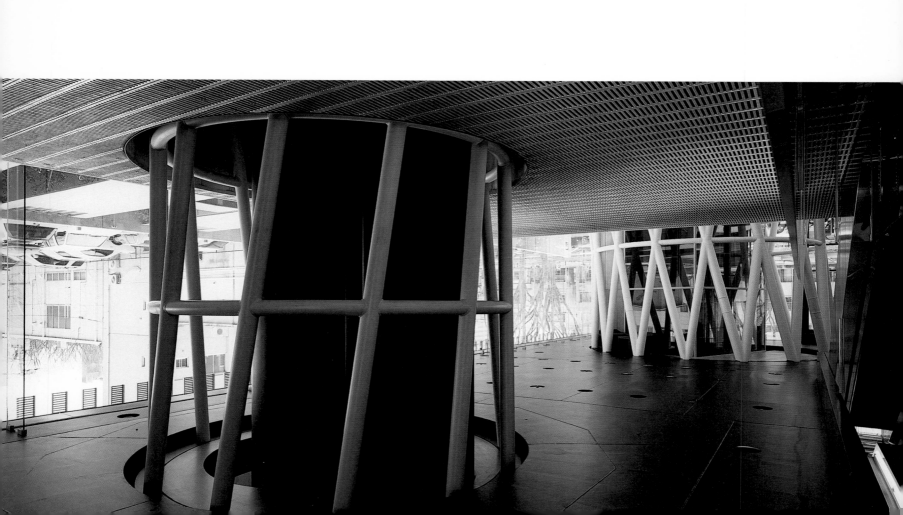

Yasuaki Onoda: It's just like a park, isn't it?

Verb: Do you have plans for future activities or problems to be solved now?

Emiko Okuyama: The most important and difficult point is to think of how to keep the 'under construction' condition always alive. People and things will come and go, but this basic concept has to remain. The philosopher Mr. Taki, who was a member of the project committee, explained how the Mediatheque is 'not a terminal, but a node', and that 'it does not offer so-called public services, but is a platform for intellectual investigation'. But it is very difficult to give shape to these ideas, and at the same time the Mediatheque has to maintain the characteristics of a public building rather than an experimental laboratory.

Verb: How do you communicate the results of this experience to the public?

Emiko Okuyama: We constantly load information into our website (http://www.smt.city.sendai.jp/). But again, it is difficult to express our thoughts on a day-to-day basis. We should be able to announce what we have learned every 1, 2 or 3 years.

Verb: Did you make The Sendai Mediatheque Concept Book as a first example of this?

Emiko Okuyama: Yes, it is a book about the ideas behind the building. From now on, we want to say what we have done, or how we have to change...

Verb: The newness of the Mediatheque not only lies in the physical building, but also in the way information is shared.

Emiko Okuyama: Mr. Eishi Katsura said that it is important to stock all of our experience in the library archives, without judging its value now because we do not have any standards to estimate its value in the future. And so we must continue to collect our experience for its eventual use someday.

Red standing sign. It works as a bookmark in the building.

Verb: Which are the main concepts behind the signage of the Sendai Mediatheque?

Yukimasa Matsuda: When I saw this building I was impressed by the tubes going through it. I compared the theme of the structure running through the building to the concept of passage in Walter Benjamin. Information is also passing through this building. Following this theme, the SMT sign is defined by a line that spreads through a square.

Also at an early stage we decided that the basic font for the different applications of the design would be Hiragino for Japanese and Frutiger for the Latin alphabet. They are both large families, easy to use, and go well together. The logo is also based on a Frutiger font.

I also designed signage and its applications for the Taisha Cultural Place, another building by Toyo Ito. When I received this commission the building was almost finished. I designed almost 500 items from the parking signs to the brochures.

Verb: Some of the signs in the Mediatheque seem to be independent from the building, like pieces of furniture.

Yukimasa Matsuda: At the request of Toyo Ito, I designed some signs that would stand out from the architecture instead of assimilating into it. They are red, and are in fact independent from the architectural elements.

Verb: After its opening, the building is being used in unexpected ways as a place to sleep or to eat. I see that as a result, some additional signs on paper have been improvised in different places.

Yukimasa Matsuda: According to the concept of this building, I think that we have to be prepared for this type of changes, to allow the signs to change.

Use

Signage

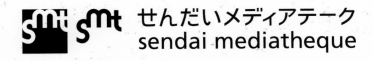

Sendai Mediatheque logo
Hiragino Kaku Gothic and Frutiger

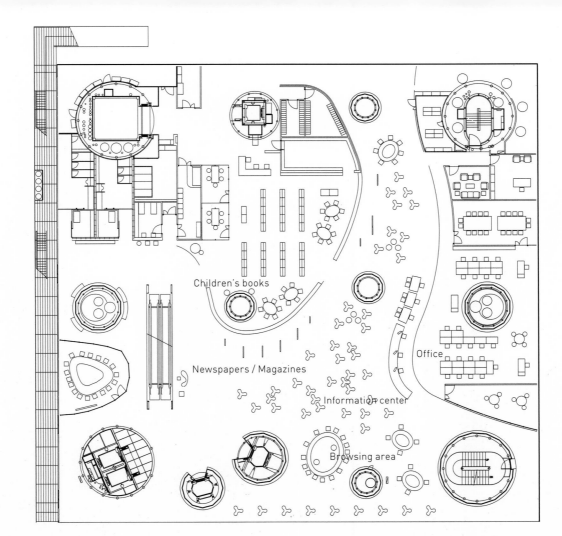

Children's books

Newspapers / Magazines

Office

Information center

Browsing area

Use

Furniture, 2nd floor
Building tour

2nd floor: Information center

0   10m   20m

Furniture, 2nd floor
Interview with Kazuyo Sejima, architect, designer of the second floor furniture

Verb: Before designing furniture for one of the floors, what impression did you have of this space?
Kazuyo Sejima: I first visited the construction site when they were finishing the slab of the fourth floor. Many craftsmen were welding the steel plates that make up the floor structure, and it really did not look like a regular construction site. Previously I had been impressed by the abstract model image in the

competition phase, and now by the strong presence of the steel tubes and slabs under construction.

Verb: What is the basic concept of your furniture, and how did you imagine the visitors would use it?

Kazuyo Sejima: The second floor of the Sendai Mediatheque does not have a specific function like some of the other floors. People come here for different purposes, like waiting in line before using an information counter, browsing through magazines, searching on the Internet, or simply meeting someone. In order to accommodate these different activities, I designed flower chairs in the shape of a trefoil. They can be combined in various ways creating different spatial organizations. One can sit on them casually, used as a big flat chair, or as a meeting chair to sit down face to face. I imagined that flowers would spread in a 50 x 50 meter floor field.

Verb: How did you choose the material?

Kazuyo Sejima: It was important to keep the sharpness of the form and make it comfortable at the same time. The seat is made of hard polyurethane colored by dip coating, and it rests on the floor as if slightly floating. The gray color was chosen from the monotone interior of the second floor.

Verb: What was your impression when you saw them in use?

Kazuyo Sejima: I was impressed by how different the space was just before the opening and on the opening day. The gallery opened, monitors were turned on, the shelves were filled, and visitors used everything, and I felt that suddenly people came to the surface, that the building disappeared and that it was replaced by people. Here I saw the new relationship that this building establishes between the users and the space. Similarly, these chairs are open to different uses and create different spatial configurations.

Verb: What is it like to design furniture as an architect?

Kazuyo Sejima: A chair is small and exists close to the human body, but if we put many chairs together, they can transform architectural space. I am very proud to be invited to do something for this project, with such a high profile from the beginning.

Use

Furniture, 2nd floor

Second floor detail plan

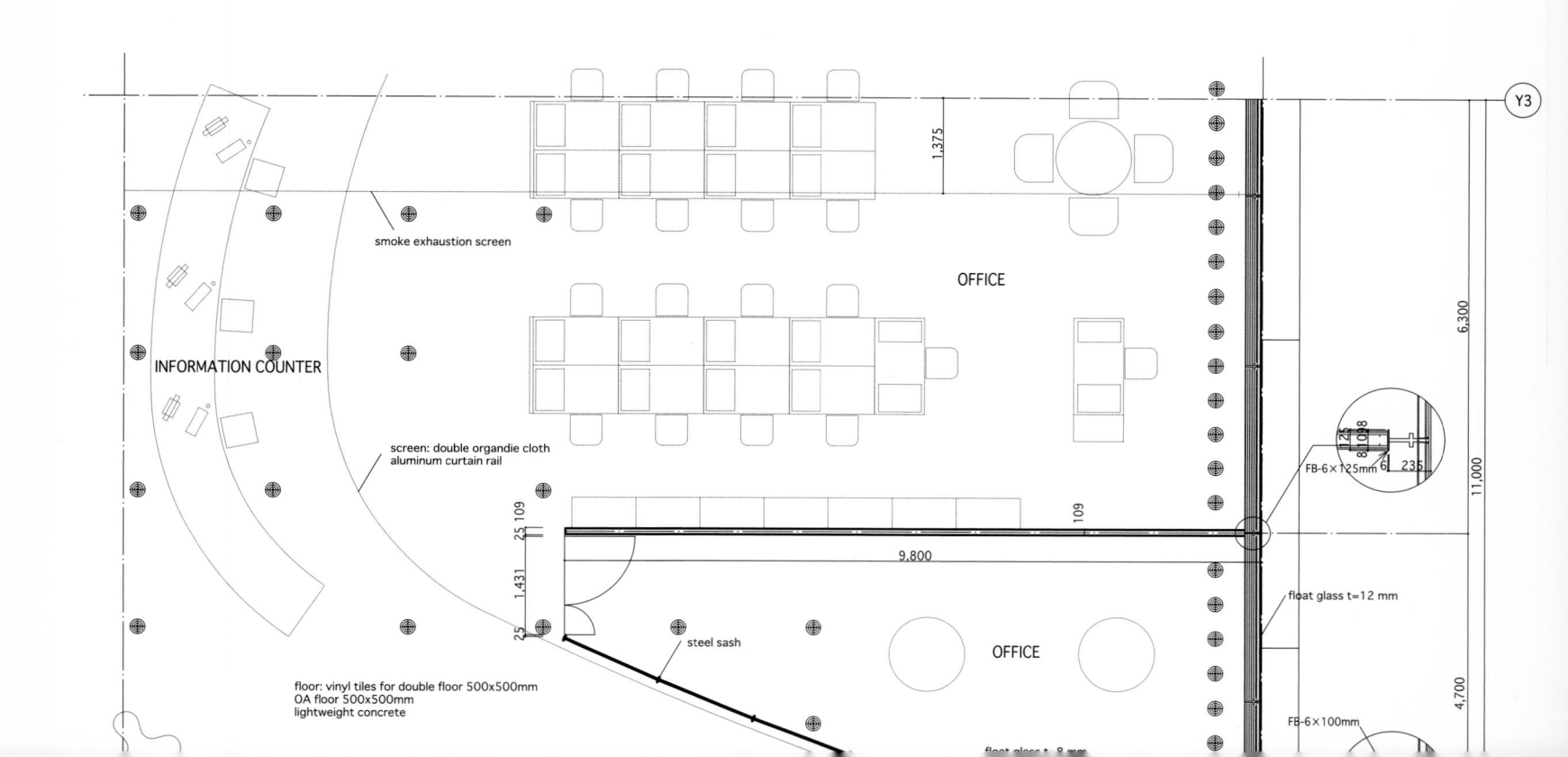

smoke exhaustion screen

OFFICE

INFORMATION COUNTER

screen: double organdie cloth
aluminum curtain rail

1.375

6.300

11.000

FB-6×125mm

float glass t=12 mm

9.800

109

25 109

1.431

25

steel sash

OFFICE

4.700

floor: vinyl tiles for double floor 500x500mm
OA floor 500x500mm
lightweight concrete

FB-6×100mm

Y3

float glass t 8 mm

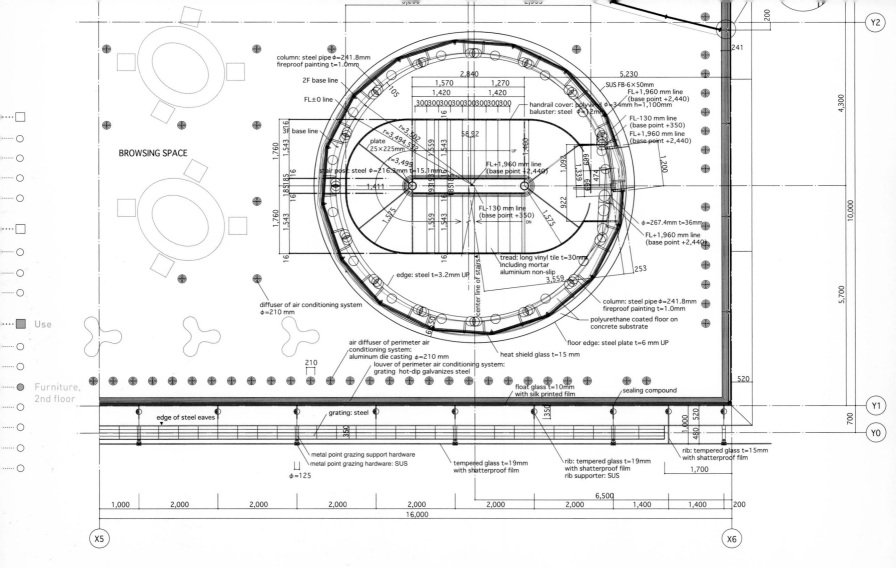

BROWSING SPACE

Use

Furniture,
2nd floor

column: steel pipe φ=241.8mm
fireproof painting t=1.0mm

2F base line

FL±0 line

3F base line

base line

stair post: steel φ=216.3mm t=15.1mm

plate
25×225mm

r=3,502
3,494,592
t=3,499

58,92

UP

handrail cover: polyvinyl φ=34mm h=1,100mm
baluster: steel t=3.2mm

SUS FB-6×50mm
FL+1,960 mm line
(base point +2,440)

FL-130 mm line
(base point +350)
FL+1,960 mm line
(base point +2,440)

FL+1,960 mm line
(base point +2,440)

FL-130 mm line
(base point +350)

DN

φ=267.4mm t=36mm

FL+1,960 mm line
(base point +2,440)

tread: long vinyl tile t=30mm
including mortar
aluminium non-slip

edge: steel t=3.2mm UP

center line of stairs

diffuser of air conditioning system
φ=210 mm

253

3,559

column: steel pipe φ=241.8mm
fireproof painting t=1.0mm

polyurethane coated floor on
concrete substrate

floor edge: steel plate t=6 mm UP

heat shield glass t=15 mm

air diffuser of perimeter air
conditioning system:
aluminum die casting φ=210 mm

louver of perimeter air conditioning system:
grating hot-dip galvanizes steel

float glass t=10mm
with silk printed film

sealing compound

grating: steel

edge of steel eaves

metal point grazing support hardware

metal point grazing hardware: SUS

φ=125

tempered glass t=19mm
with shatterproof film

rib: tempered glass t=19mm
with shatterproof film
rib supporter: SUS

rib: tempered glass t=15mm
with shatterproof film

1,700

Y2

241

4,300

10,000

5,700

520

Y1

Y0

700

5,230

210

6,500

1,000   2,000   2,000   2,000   2,000   2,000   2,000   1,400   1,400   200

16,000

X5

X6

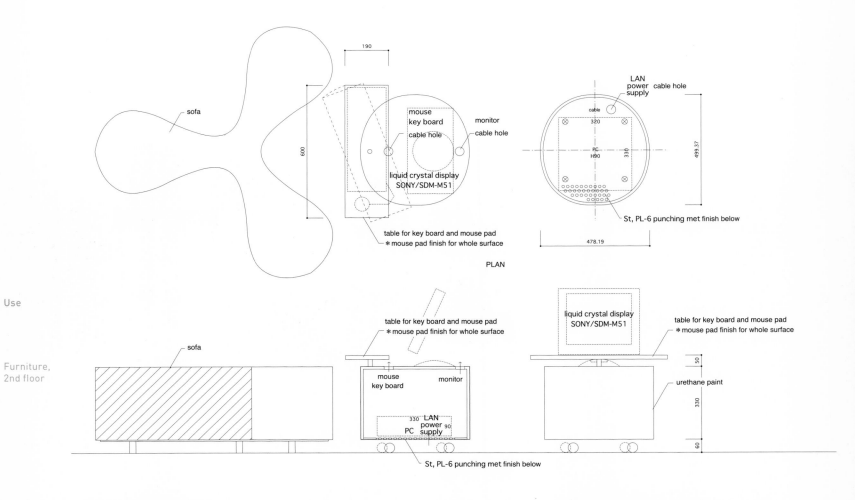

sofa

190

600

mouse
key board

cable hole

monitor

cable hole

liquid crystal display
SONY/SDM-M51

table for key board and mouse pad
*mouse pad finish for whole surface

PLAN

LAN
power
supply

cable hole

cable

320

PC
H90

330

499.37

478.19

St, PL-6 punching met finish below

Use

Furniture,
2nd floor

sofa

table for key board and mouse pad
*mouse pad finish for whole surface

mouse
key board

monitor

330 LAN
PC power 90
supply

St, PL-6 punching met finish below

SECTION

liquid crystal display
SONY/SDM-M51

table for key board and mouse pad
*mouse pad finish for whole surface

urethane paint

50

330

60

ELEVATION

Browsing table and sofa
designed by Kazuyo Sejima & Associates

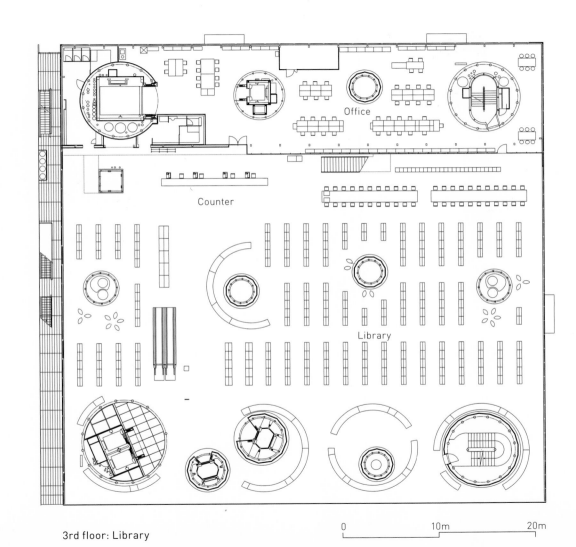

Office

Counter

Library

3rd floor: Library

0   10m   20m

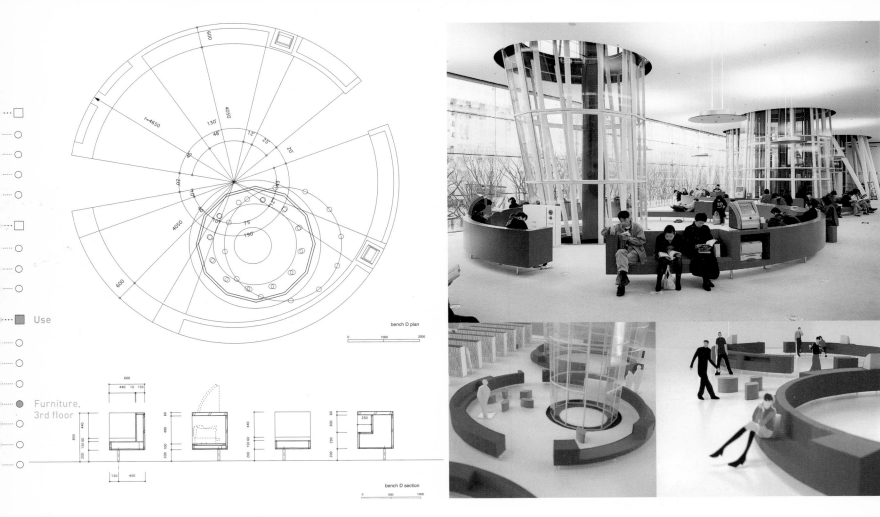

Red-ring bench designed by KTA
(Yoshiaki Tezuka + Hirono Koike)

Use

Furniture,
3rd floor

bench D plan

0   1000   2000

bench D section

0   500   1000

Furniture, 3rd floor
K.T. Architecture, designers of the library furniture

Toyo Ito asked us to design the Mediatheque's library furniture following our previous collaboration as the furniture designers in the Taisha Bunka Place in Shimane. Our basic approach for the Mediatheque was to avoid designing objects or specific shapes, but rather to design a 'place' in which to read books comfortably that would exist in relation with the architecture of the tubes.

White bookshelves

The shelves are made of fire-resistant steel and are based on ready-made shelves in order to cut down production costs. They have no backboards and are composed of the thinnest members, so as to avoid the generally oppressive feeling of many libraries, and to open the views through the shelves. By means of these simple devices we intended to contradict the massiveness of conventional bookshelves and create a bright space in which users would freely wander amidst a forest of books, with natural sunlight coming from the tubes.

Red-ring bench

The librarians asked us to design a specific piece of furniture for each function, which would have originated an overcrowded counter space. We decided instead to reduce the number of items, and worked on a large-scaled furniture piece of simple geometry that could respond to many functions, hopefully also to unforeseen requirements. The result is the red-ring bench that has been placed around 5 tubes on the southern edge of the floor. These benches work as reading seats, writing desks, supports for the computers and printers, showcases, and display bookshelves. As they can be used from either the interior or the exterior sides of the rings, users can choose the direction they face and the distance they keep from other users.

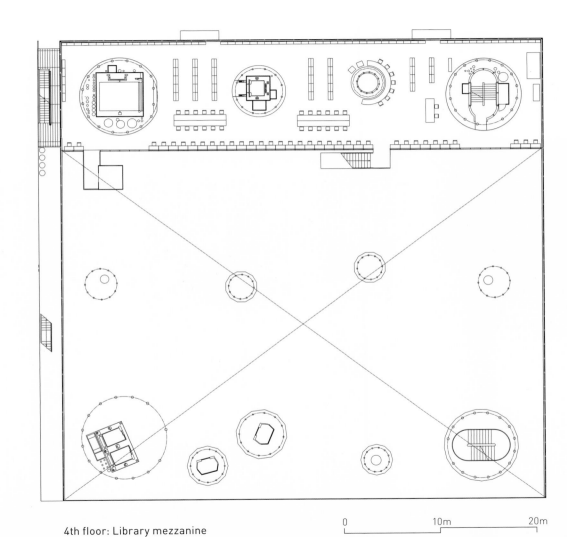

Use

Furniture, 3rd floor
Building tour

4th floor: Library mezzanine

0   10m   20m

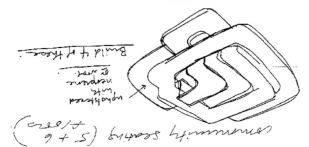

Bench around the tube and multi-bench
designed by Karim Rashid

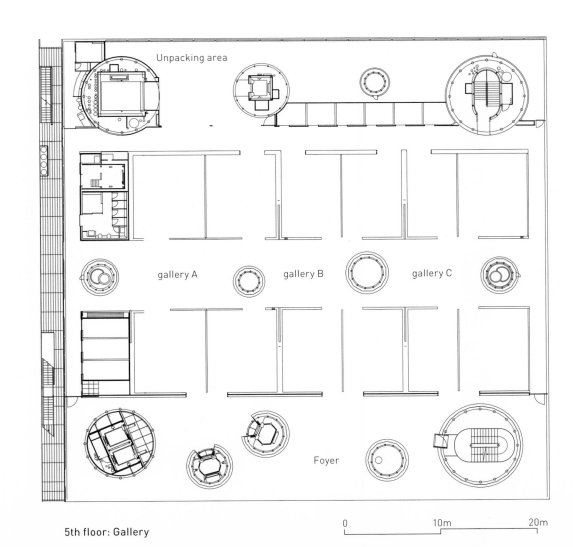

Unpacking area

gallery A   gallery B   gallery C

Foyer

Use

Building tour

5th floor: Gallery

0   10m   20m

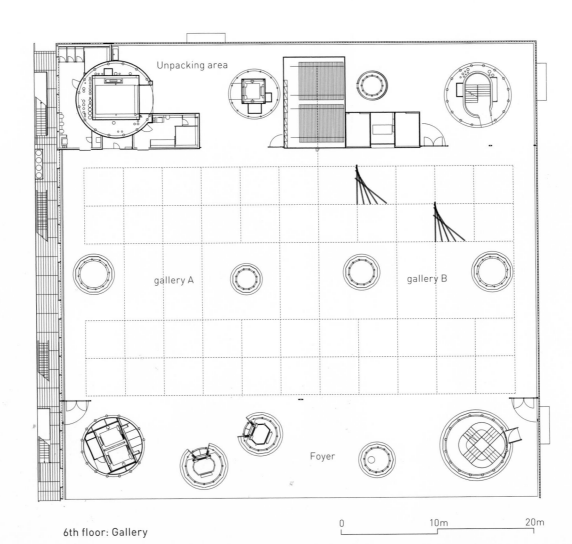

Use

Building tour

Unpacking area

gallery A

gallery B

Foyer

0   10m   20m

6th floor: Gallery

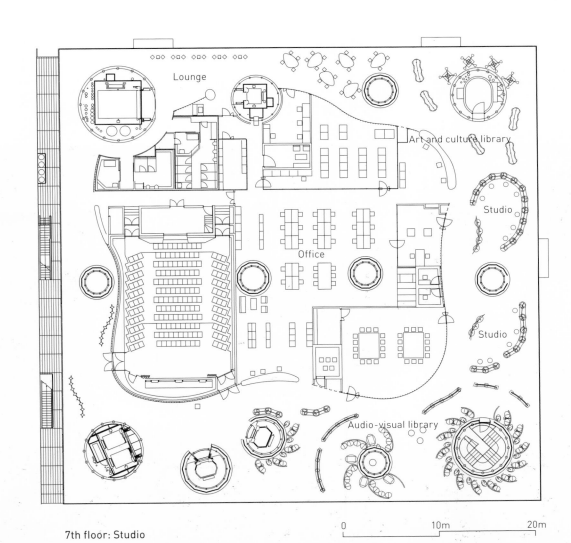

7th floor: Studio

Lounge

Art and culture library

Studio

Office

Studio

Audio-visual library

Use

Building tour

0   10m   20m

Verb: What is your job in the Mediatheque?

Naoto Ogawa: I am in charge of the workshops and of other events involving computers in the 7th floor theater and studio space. I work here as a computer media specialist.

Verb: What is the process behind organizing a workshop?

Naoto Ogawa: There are 3 types of workshops: the projects prepared by Sendai Mediatheque, the external projects, and the collaboration projects. For example, we did a workshop on city planning in Sendai with architecture students, and another one about how to film the festivals in Sendai for which I had to give a class on how to use the equipment. We basically lease the spaces and the equipment. Sometimes we organize projections in the theater of films which are not usually shown in the cinemas, like old Japanese movies shot in Sendai, architectural films by Le Corbusier, or documentaries on work that is exhibited in the gallery. We have also helped local directors to self-produce a movie by hiring out the camera and the computer equipment.

Verb: And there are also workshops on how to use specific computer programs.

Naoto Ogawa: Yes, there are workshops for specific groups, for instance teaching programs for the blind, or workshops for seniors who teach other seniors how to use a computer. This is a workshop called 'senior net', which was established to raise computer literacy among senior citizens. We also teach a general introduction to different types of software called 'application tour'. One of the recent products of this workshop is the brochure for this month's movie program at the Mediatheque, a monographic program of films from our neighboring Yamagata prefecture, with which we are planning a joint film festival. The excellent design of this brochure was made by the workshop students using Illustrator and Photoshop. And as I said we also have external projects which originate anywhere, not only in Sendai. We recently hosted 'Movement', an exhibition covering an international selection of graphic design works, and we had to work 24 hours a day... There are still few curators who know how to use a computer.

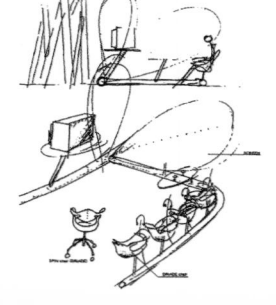

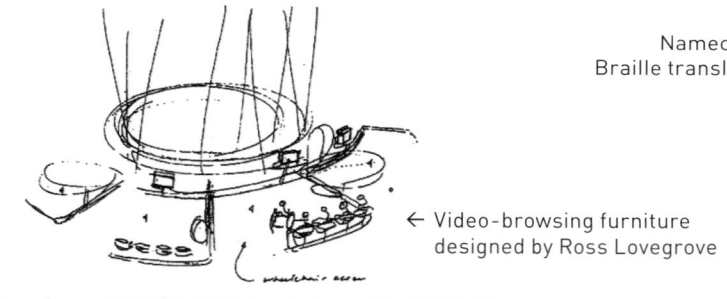

← Video-browsing furniture
designed by Ross Lovegrove

Namecard with →
Braille transliteration

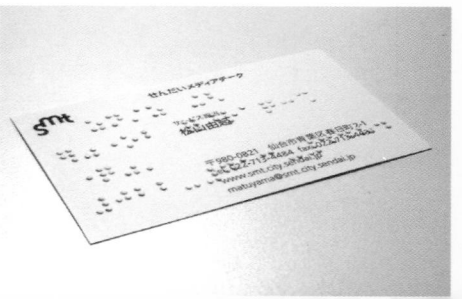

Verb: And how did you start to work here?

Naoto Ogawa: While I was studying art management at university I did some sociological research on museums, developed a big interest in film and acquired some knowledge and experience on computers. I got this job right after I graduated from university.

Verb: Apart from the free space for the workshops or 'application tours', there is also a video library here.

Naoto Ogawa: The concept of the studio on this 7th floor was decided in the early stage of planning, but we did not have any concrete program until just before the opening. We now have a new video division of the city library. I selected almost every item, with the criterion of covering a standard academic or artistic range of works as well as complementing the collections in other libraries and what is usually found in commercial shops. After the opening we also accept users' requests.

Verb: The Sendai Mediatheque has very long opening hours for a public facility in Japan. Do you have special working hours?

Naoto Ogawa: We have two different work shifts. One from 8:00 to 17:00, and the other from 14:00 to 22:00. Personally, I work from 10:00 to... 25:00 or 26:00. There's never enough time.

Yuki Matsuyama, receptionist to attend the blind, Sendai Mediatheque staff

Verb: Could you tell us about your work here?

Yuki Matsuyama: I offer various services to vision-impaired people. I work on Braille, or read any type of printed matter face to face to the blind. Other libraries also have works on Braille or tape recordings of books, with which we have set up a network of libraries that gives priority to immediacy. At present, we mainly translate or read periodicals and the SMT brochures. We call ourselves the 'barrier-free team', consisting of 2 people who can help the blind, 2 who can help the deaf and use sign language, and the program coordinator. An average of 5 handicapped people per year visit the other public library in this prefecture, but here it is approximately one person per week.

Use

Working in SMT

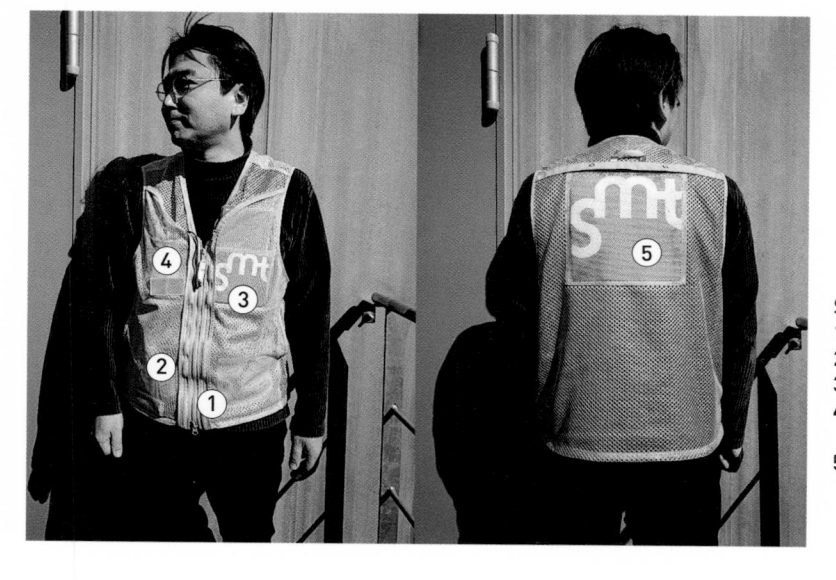

Sign vest functions
1. Zipper can be opened from both up and down.
2. Zipper for inside pocket (4 pockets)
3. Pocket
4. Reflection sign: the smt sign can be seen from any angle, and works as a reflector, too.
5. Back pocket for smt sign with snap closure. The sign is made of cloth printed in red or blue. The big one is for the back, and the small one is for the front.

Wearable sign
Interview with Kosuke Tsumura, fashion designer

Verb: How did you start to get involved in the design of the 'wearable sign' for the Sendai Mediatheque?
Kosuke Tsumura: Mr. Akira Suzuki requested my participation. From the beginning, it was designed not as a so-called uniform, but as something that would distinguish the people who work here from the visitors. This is usually done by means of suits, or jackets and trousers of the same design to make all employees uniform. But in this case all that was needed was a distinctive mark. The concept of 'wearable sign' originated from this realization. It could have been a sash or an armband, but I designed instead a vest that would also have other functions.
I made the sign big enough for old people to recognize it easily, and designed several pockets for brochures or a mobile phone. It is made of mesh cloth, a semi-transparent material, so that all these things inside

the pockets are vaguely seen through it. The color is gray to match with the building. The employee's own jacket or sweater can also be seen under this semi-transparent gray vest, so as not to separate him or her too much from the visitors. The apron for library clerks was an exception, because it was necessary to make it opaque in order to protect their own clothes from dust when they were carrying the books. It is made of a mixed fiber of kevlar and cotton, in the same shade of gray.

Verb: Could you tell us about the 'Final Home' project, which I think uses the same concept of the pockets? From the name it sounds like an architectural project.

Kosuke Tsumura: I used the term 'home' instead of 'house' because it communicates a sense of security. Here I thought of the pockets as personal containers, for instance as a space for a stuffed doll during an earthquake. They can also be used in much more functional ways, like being stuffed it with newspaper to protect us from the cold wind. But my intention was that the pockets would be used for much more spiritual things, also in a humorous way. We read a book and gain some knowledge, and the physical book is torn apart and put inside pockets as simple paper representing the new information inside us.

Verb: Why do you design 'pockets' for these projects?

Kosuke Tsumura: The pocket is a space between the surface and the lining cloth which I wanted to put to use. In a house, there is usually an insulating material between the interior and exterior walls, and probably this insulation is not necessary in all seasons and the space it occupies could sometimes be used for storage. I think that the most radical concept of the Sendai Mediatheque is that it accepts new ways of using space, leaving it up to the users to find out how to do it. It is open to discovery.

I expect the users to enjoy finding new ways to wear their clothes. Fashion can be connected to fascism, if the user is forced to accept the designers' style or concept. If one style is in fashion and everybody follows it, it becomes a uniform. And the designer is guilty of aiming only at maximum consumption.

I think it is important for us to design products with a public awareness, both regarding the use of materials and the use assigned to our products.

Use

Wearable sign

Use

Building tour

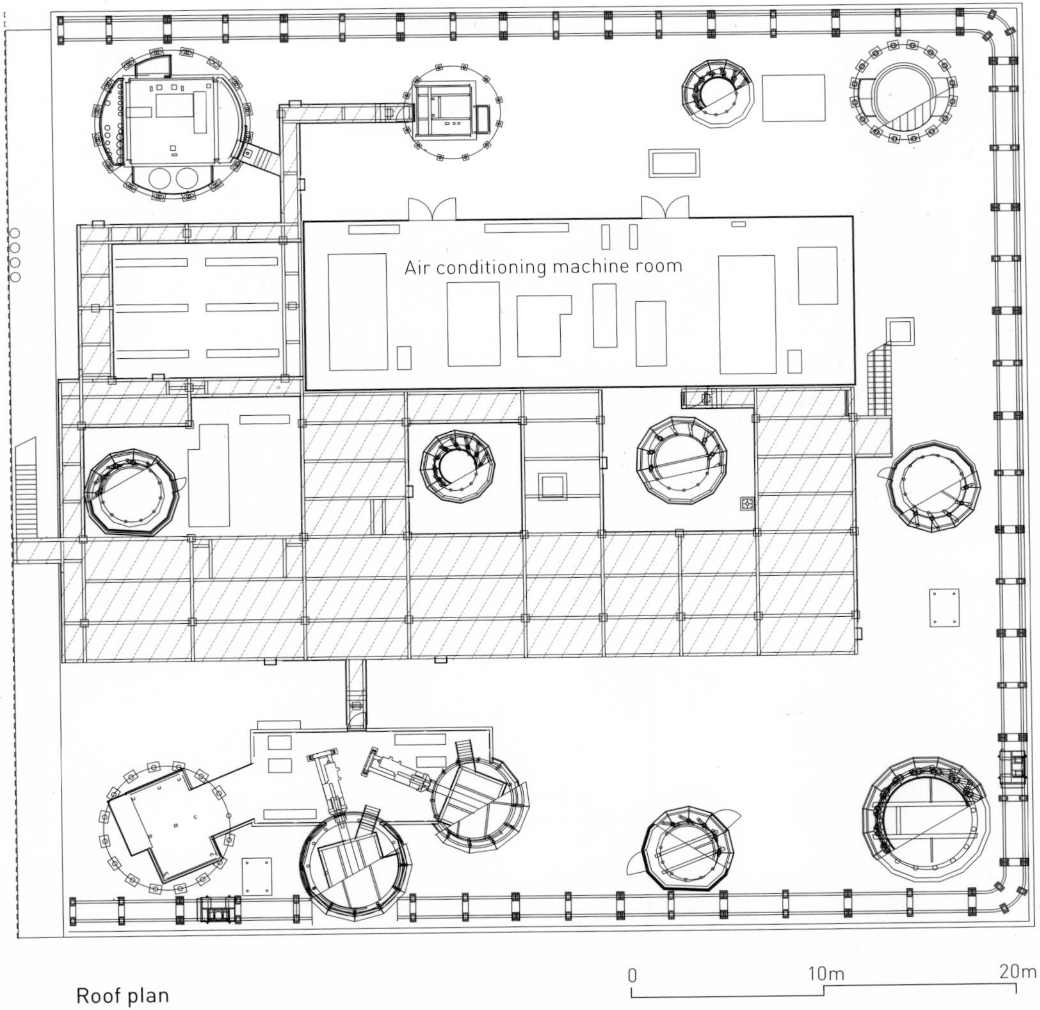

Air conditioning machine room

Roof plan

0   10m   20m

Verb: By naming this building a 'Mediatheque', Arata Isozaki and the competition jury seemed to be looking for a public facility that would respond to the present and future requirements of the information age. A possible approach would have been to use the latest building technologies or to design simple containers that could be continuously transformed.

Toyo Ito: I tried to answer in two simultaneous ways. Regarding the program, we looked at how the use of the computer affects the organization of a library or of a museum. And regarding the image of the space, the approach was to suggest an architectural metaphor of computer or electronic technology, just like 20th-century architects based the image of their architecture on metaphors of the machine age. I thought of referring to communication networks as something fluid, like water streams, to produce an artificial nature rather than architecture. When I first tried to draw this concept I rejected the idea of spatial partitions or individual rooms, so I tried to make 'places' instead of 'rooms'. These places are defined by furniture, not by walls, and coexist with the tubes reminiscent of natural streams or forests.This building is not only a center for new media, but for any kind of media coexisting side by side. There is a library and a gallery for the visualization of very classical media like books and paintings, and conference rooms full of computers. The building becomes a sort of 'supermarket' or 'convenience store' of media.

Verb: Not only does media exist inside the Sendai Mediatheque, but also the Mediatheque is present in the media. Long before its completion, this building was well known through various types of media such as newspapers, magazines, and the SMT website.

Use

After the opening

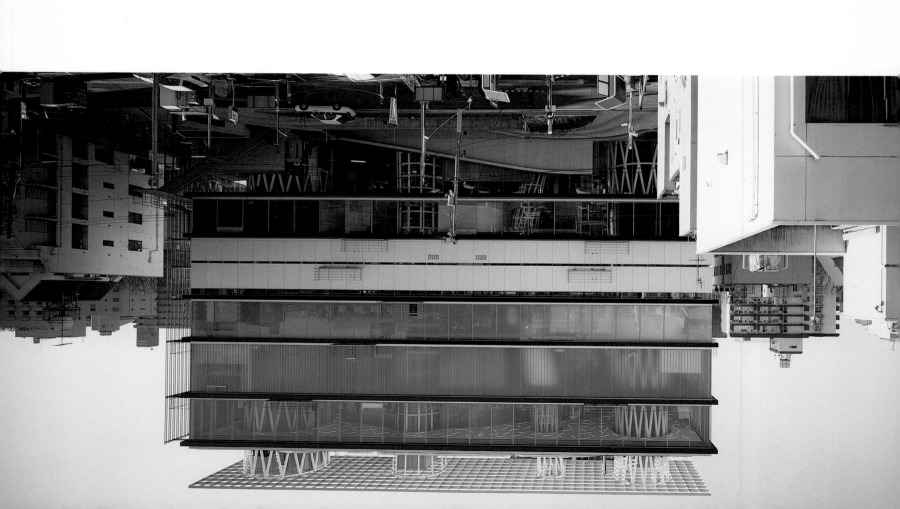

Toyo Ito: The first photograph of the competition model had a strong impact. Besides Arata Isozaki, the other jury members were also specialists in different issues relating to the building, and not government officials or representatives. This is the reason why I dared to present such a simple and pure image for the building, without any walls or clearly recognizable architectural symbols. I knew that they would understand. The model showed the image of something like trees, overlapped with an architectural image of columns. But after the competition, the image of the model was shown to all the people concerned in this project, from the craftsmen to the government officials. And I think it worked.

Verb: Akira Suzuki told me that the main decision regarding the program was to avoid fixing it, to leave its future definition completely open. Didn't you have to face a certain opposition during the design or building process to the absence of walls as a way of guaranteeing this 'openness'?

Toyo Ito: I never wanted to put walls in the building, and in this case the tubes are absolute obstacles to the existence of walls. In fact, the local newspapers wrote that the tubes were spatially disturbing... Thanks to the tubes, we could go on until the end without building the walls. And finally, the spaces were defined by means of furniture and its placement. It the end, the furniture had to solve every problem.

Verb: Why did you not design the furniture yourself but decide to commission it to other designers?

Toyo Ito: From the very beginning I thought of leaving the whole design of each floor to a different designer. We used different materials and different lighting on each floor, but in the end all of this diversity seems to originate from the idea of one single designer.

Verb: Does this mean that you also took part in the way the furniture is laid out?

Toyo Ito: Yes, we did. There were very long discussions between the designers, the programmers and my office.

Use

After the opening

Verb: Can the furniture layout change in the future according to changes in the Mediatheque's program?

Toyo Ito: It could happen. Design, construction and use have no borders between them. I am interested in the way these three moments can become totally overlapped, and how we can embody such a situation from beginning to end.

Verb: What is your role in the future of the Sendai Mediatheque?

Toyo Ito: I am still observing what is happening there, and in fact I think that I can still be involved in the future. Ms. Okuyama seems to be willing to accept my advice, and she says that it is very difficult to control the entire process. The building has attracted a lot of media attention and it seems to be fulfilling its goals, but the next step is to think of strategies to generate more creative activities. And it is very important to constantly bring new people and new activities into the building so as to avoid possible feelings of self-satisfaction or the perception of conclusion.

Verb: Do you think that SMT will become a reference for future 'Mediatheques' in other cities?

Toyo Ito: It is possible, I think. And the reason why a lot of people like this building is the relaxed atmosphere inside. This feeling is needed in community facilities. It is possible to realize this kind of space anywhere, not as a consequence of the program but as an outcome of the design process. In this sense, this building can exist only in Sendai, and different buildings will be built in different cities. We have been using this building from the beginning, using it while designing it, and continuing to design it after we have built it. When we make a public facility, the most important thing is to think about how we can introduce this idea of continuity into the process of the project.

Use

After the opening

publishing list

before the competition

19940405	建設工業新聞	Tokyo
19940425	建設工業新聞	Tokyo
19940713	建設工業新聞	Tokyo
19940720	朝日新聞	Tokyo
19940720	読売新聞	Tokyo
19940720	河北新報	Sendai
19940720	日刊建設新聞	Tokyo
19940720	日刊建設新聞	Tokyo
19940720	建設工業新聞	Tokyo
199407	読売新聞	Tokyo
199408	東北ジャーナル	Sendai
19940903	河北新報	Sendai
19940906	建設産業新聞	Tokyo
19940906	建設新聞	Sendai
19940906	日刊建設工業新聞	Tokyo
19940906	建設工業新聞	Tokyo
19940906	日刊工業新聞	Tokyo
19940907	建設通信新聞	Tokyo
19941010	日経アーキテクチュア	Tokyo
19941011	河北新報	Sendai

competition entry

19941102	日刊建設工業新聞	Tokyo
19941102	日刊建設工業新聞	Tokyo
19941102	建設新聞	Sendai
19941102	河北新報	Sendai
19941102	河北新報	Sendai
19941115	朝日新聞	Tokyo
19950215	産経新聞	Tokyo
19950228	河北新報	Sendai
19950310	河北新報	Sendai
19950314	河北新報	Sendai
19950315	毎日新聞	Tokyo
19950315	朝日新聞	Tokyo
19950316	日刊建設新聞	Tokyo
19950316	日刊建設産業新聞	Tokyo
19950316	河北新報	Sendai
19950316	日刊建設工業新聞	Tokyo

basic design

19950324	河北新報	Sendai
19950324	朝日新聞	Tokyo
199503	JA	Tokyo
199503	せんだいメディアテーク設計競技記録	Sendai
199503	JA THE JAPAN ARCHITECTURE	Tokyo
19950420	建設通信新聞	Tokyo
19950420	河北抄	Sendai
19950424	日経アーキテクチュア	Tokyo
199504	GA DOCUMENT INTERNATIONAL'95	Tokyo
199504	東北ジャーナル	Sendai
199504	GA DOCUMENT INTERNATIONAL'95	Tokyo
19950603	河北新報	Sendai
19950605	河北新報	Sendai
19950607	河北新報	Sendai
19950612	河北新報	Sendai
19950627	河北新報	Sendai
199507	GA JAPAN Global Architecture Japan	Tokyo
199507	公共建築	Tokyo
19950829	河北新報	Sendai
19950830	建設通信新聞	Tokyo
19951031	河北新報	Sendai
19951116	毎日新聞	Tokyo
19951118	河北新報	Sendai
19951118	私の選んだ一品	Tokyo
19951124	河北新報	Sendai
19951127	建設通信新聞	Osaka
199511	Techniques&Architecture	Paris
1995	Lotus93	Milan
1995	GA JAPAN Global Architecture Japan	Tokyo
199601	イミダス96	Tokyo
199601	InterCommunication	Tokyo
19960104	朝日新聞	Tokyo
19960119	仙台リビング	Sendai
199603	東北大学建築学報	Sendai
199603	AIT: Intelligente Architektur 4	Leinfelden-Echterdingen

199604	at Architecture Today	Tokyo
19960418	建設通信新聞	Tokyo
199605	at Atchitecture Today	Tokyo
199605	構造設計の詩法	Tokyo
19960520	河北新報	Sendai
19960613	朝日新聞	Tokyo
19960617	建設通信新聞	Tokyo
19960624	建設通信新聞	Tokyo
19960630	La Vanguardia Magazine	Barcelona
199606	Projeto Design	Sao Paulo
199606	D'Architectures	Paris
199606	La Vanguardia Magazine	Barcelona
199606	建築と社会	Tokyo
199606	petit Journal de l'expositon/Centre Georges Pompidou	Paris
199608	Zlaty Rez	Praha
199608	河北新報	Sendai
199609	6th International architecture exhibition	Milan
19961028	河北新報	Sendai
19961104	日経アーキテクチュア	Tokyo
199611	新建築	Tokyo
19961216	河北新報	Sendai
19961224	建設通信新聞	Tokyo
19961225	建設通信新聞	Tokyo
19961226	建設通信新聞	Tokyo
19961228	河北新報	Sendai
19961228	河北新報	Sendai
199612	仙台っこ	Tokyo
19970106	朝日新聞	Tokyo
19970108	建設通信新聞	Tokyo
19970213	建設通信新聞	Tokyo
19970224	建設通信新聞	Tokyo
199703	室内	Tokyo
19970328	建設通信新聞	Tokyo
199704	公共建築	Tokyo
19970402	河北新報	Sendai
19970409	河北新報	Sendai
19970416	河北新報	Sendai
199705	Cultura	Mexico
199705	THE VIRTUAL ARCHITECTURE	Tokyo
199705	Contemporary Architecture 13	
19970509	河北新報	Sendai
19970522	建設通信新聞	Tokyo

Date	Publication	City
19970522	毎日新聞	Tokyo
19970625	河北新報 夕 杜の都３	Sendai
199706	L'art de l'ingenieur	Paris
199706	建築雑誌	Tokyo
199706	日本経済新聞	Tokyo
19970710	建設通信新聞	Tokyo
19970714	建設通信新聞	Tokyo
19970724	建設通信新聞	Tokyo
199707	Thesis	Munich
19970901	建設通信新聞	
19970901	建設通信新聞	Tokyo
19970918	建設通信新聞	Tokyo
19970930	建設通信新聞	Tokyo
19971022	建設通信新聞	Tokyo
19971111	建設通信新聞	Tokyo
199711	Ideal Architecture	Pusan
19971120	朝日新聞	Tokyo
19971203	河北新報	Sendai
19971217	河北新報	Sendai
19971226	建設通信新聞	Tokyo
199712	東北ジャーナル	Tokyo
199712	CITY&LIFE	Tokyo
1997	2G	Barcelona
1997	宮城教育大学紀要	Sendai
1997	Lotus 93	Milan
1997	Harvard Design Magazine Vol.6	Cambridge
1997	Columbia Documents of Architecture and Theory	New York
19980120	河北新報	Sendai
19980120	朝日新聞	Tokyo

construction started

Date	Publication	City
19980121	建設通信新聞	Tokyo
19980129	建設通信新聞	Tokyo
19980205	建設通信新聞	Tokyo
19980206	建設通信新聞	Tokyo
19980216	建設通信新聞	Tokyo
19980226	建設通信新聞	Tokyo
199803	建築・夢の軌跡	Tokyo
199803	DETAIL Review of Architecture	Munchen
19980301	河北新報	Sendai
19980315	河北新報	Sendai
19980317	建設通信新聞	Tokyo
19980322	河北新報	Sendai
19980322	朝日新聞	Tokyo
19980330	建設通信新聞	Tokyo
19980402	建設通信新聞	Tokyo
19980619	河北新報	Sendai
19980709	建設通信新聞	Tokyo
19980820	建設通信新聞	Tokyo
19980907	日本経済新聞	Tokyo
19980928	河北新聞	Sendai
19981012	河北新報	Sendai
19981027	東京読売新聞	Tokyo
19981104	建設通信新聞	Tokyo
19981204	河北新報	Sendai
1998	El Croquis Worlds one	Madrid
1998	summa+36	Buenos Aires
1998	FRAME 8 vol.3	Amsterdam
199901	GA JAPAN Global Architecture Japan	Tokyo
19990111	日経アーキテクチュア ６３１	Tokyo
19990203	建設通信新聞	Tokyo
19990203	朝日新聞	Tokyo
19990216	建設通信新聞	Tokyo
19990225	河北新報	Sendai
199903	gap	Tokyo
19990303	建設通信新聞	Tokyo
19990310	10+1	Tokyo
19990318	朝日新聞	Tokyo
19990320	河北新報	Sendai
19990323	建設通信新聞	Tokyo
19990324	建設通信新聞	Tokyo
19990410	CASA BRUTUS	Tokyo
19990416	建設通信新聞	Tokyo
19990425	朝日新聞	Tokyo
199905	GA JAPAN Global Architecture Japan	Tokyo
19990503	河北新報	Sendai
199906	建築文化	Tokyo
199906	河北新報	Sendai
19990709	建設通信新聞	Tokyo
19990715	建設通信新聞	Tokyo
19990806	建設通信新聞	Tokyo
19990910	建設通信新聞社	Tokyo
19990912	河北新報	Sendai
199909	流行通信	Tokyo
199909	GA JAPAN Global Architecture Japan	Tokyo
19991010	きゅうぷらす	Tokyo
19991112	読売新聞	Tokyo
19991125	朝日新聞	Tokyo
19991216	朝日新聞	Tokyo
1999	arkitektur " Japan genom 5 Forkhemmets form Inredningar	Stockholm
20000101	河北新報	Sendai
20000129	仙台リビング	Sendai
20000129	仙台リビング	Sendai
20000210	河北新報	Sendai
20000229	河北新報	Sendai
20000229	Filmnetwork	Tokyo
20000314	河北新報	Sendai
20000315	建設産業新聞社	Tokyo
20000321	マルチメディア社会と変容する 文化3 想像と創造の未来	Tokyo
20000322	建設通信新聞	Sendai
20000322	中国新聞	Hiroshima
200003	東京デザインセンター・インフォメーション Spring 2000	Tokyo
200003	2000仙台市職員募集ガイド	Sendai
20000407	建設通信新聞	Sendai
20000417	日経アーキテクチャー	Tokyo
200004	de Architect	Den Haag
20000501	東北ジャーナル	Sendai
20000501	美術手帖	Tokyo
20000501	仙台市政だより	Sendai
20000515	BRUTUS	Tokyo

building construction completed

Date	Publication	City
20000701	まちあるきマップ定禅寺通	Sendai
20000819	河北新報	Sendai
20000822	朝日新聞	Tokyo
20001001	建築ジャーナル	Tokyo
20001025	SWITCH	Tokyo
20001028	よみうりCha!	Tokyo

Date	Publication	City
20001028	河北新報	Sendai
20001201	仙台っこ	Sendai
20001205	読売新聞	Tokyo
20001210	電気設備学会誌	Tokyo
20001215	月刊ミュゼ	Tokyo
20001228	りらく1月号	Sendai

opened

Date	Publication	City
20010100	京都リビング	Kyoto
20010101	東北ジャーナル	Sendai
20010105	日刊工業新聞	Tokyo
20010105	月刊不動産流通	Tokyo
20010117	せんだいタウン情報	Sendai
20010119	シティリビング	Sendai
20010120	河北新報	Sendai
20010121	朝日新聞	Tokyo
20010122	日経アーキテクチュア	Tokyo
20010124	朝日新聞	Tokyo
20010124	読売新聞	Tokyo
20010124	河北新報	Sendai
20010125	河北新報	Sendai
20010125	週刊るぽ	Sendai
20010125	建設通信新聞	Tokyo
20010125	地域創造レター	Tokyo
20010127	りらく2月号	Sendai
20010130	朝日ウィル	Sendai
20010131	せんだいタウン情報	Sendai
20010203	日本経済新聞	Tokyo
20010205	デザインの現場	Tokyo
20010208	河北新報	Sendai
20010211	産経新聞	Tokyo
20010216	別冊ガイドブック「まるごと仙台マガジン」	Sendai
20010220	河北アルファ	Sendai
20010220	あいだ	Toyama
20010224	よみうりCha!	Tokyo
20010225	シティ情報ふくしま	Sendai
20010225	PJ仙台マガジン	Sendai
200102	杜の伝言版ゆるる	Sendai
200102	ARCHIS	Rotterdam
20010301	ギャラリー2001	Tokyo
20010301	岩沼屋"花散里だより"	Sendai
20010301	新建築3月号	Tokyo
20010301	GA JAPAN Global Architecture Japan	Tokyo
20010301	建築文化ディテール別冊	Tokyo
20010301	建築文化別冊	Tokyo
20010301	商店建築3月号	Tokyo
20010301	室内3月号	Tokyo
20010301	なごみ	Kyoto
20010301	建築技術3月号	Tokyo
20010301	カーサブルータス	Tokyo
20010301	月刊とうほく財界	Sendai
20010305	日経アーキテクチュア	Tokyo
20010305	日経アーキテクチュア	Tokyo
20010305	日経アーキテクチュア	Tokyo
20010311	新美術新聞	Tokyo
20010311	SESAME	Tokyo
20010315	河北新報	Sendai
20010316	たべる宮城おいしいおでかけ	Sendai
20010317	日経流通新聞	Tokyo
20010317	中日新聞	Nagoya
20010321	仙台市職労	Sendai
20010322	図書館の学校 4月号	Tokyo
20010322	インターネット	Tokyo
20010324	よみうりCha!	Tokyo
20010325	仙台経済界 臨時増刊号「Senkey 1 2001春号」	Sendai
20010331	仙台わがまち	Sendai
20010103	de Architect	
200103	財務時報	Sendai
200103	domus	Milan
20010401	AXIS	Tokyo
20010401	Senkey1	Sendai
20010401	InterCommunication	Tokyo
20010401	建築文化	Tokyo
20010401	教育せんだい	Sendai
20010405	帝国タイムス	Tokyo
20010405	帝国ニュース・トウホクバン	Tokyo
20010405	mt(LIVES-MT 005)	
20010406	ICANOF	Hachinohe
20010407	エル・デコ	Tokyo
20010412	3M Profile	Tokyo
20010412	河北新報	Sendai
20010420	はなやま	Sendai
20010421	Inter National Press	
20010425	てんぴょう	Tokyo
20010425	ロジマガ	Sendai
20010425	図書館の学校 5月号	Tokyo
200104	印刷界	Tokyo
20010501	広報しおがま	Shiogama
20010504	日本教育新聞	Tokyo
20010505	東北レジャー情報	Sendai
20010509	せんだいタウン情報	Sendai
20010511	SESAME	Tokyo
20010515	JIAnews	Tokyo
20010516	河北新報	Sendai
20010518	design plex	Tokyo
20010520	htwi 6月号	Tokyo
20010523	図書館の学校	Tokyo
200105	青葉区ガイドマップ	Sendai
200105	仙台はなもく	Sendai
200105	werk,bauen+wohnen	Zurich
20010601	Confort	Tokyo
20010601	GA JAPAN Global Architecture Japan	Tokyo
20010601	STUDIO VOICE	Tokyo
20010601	装苑	Tokyo
20010601	仙台っこ	Sendai
20010601	流行通信	Tokyo
20010614	河北ウィークリー	Sendai
20010614	まっぷるマガジン仙台・松島 2002年版	Sendai
20010619	河北新報	Sendai
20010628	りらく	Sendai
200106	石垣2001年6月号	Tokyo
20010701	インターコミュニケーション	Tokyo
20010701	エレベータ界	Tokyo
20010701	SILKROAD	
20010703	河北新報	Sendai
20010704	月刊チンタイ東北版	Tokyo
20010710	変貌する美術館	Kyoto
20010715	生涯学習空間	Tokyo
20010718	design plex	Tokyo
20010718	Newsweek7/18	Tokyo
20010720	ぱれっと	Sendai
20010725	アート・ドキュメンテーション通信	Kyoto
200107	Kawasaki News〔夏号〕	Tokyo
200107	art4d	Bangkok

Date	Title	Location
200108	仙台コンベンション施設ガイド	Sendai
20010801	月刊マナビィ 8月号	Tokyo
20010801	建築文化 8月号	Tokyo
20010801	私の青空/エアーニッポン機内誌	Tokyo
20010831	河北新報	Sendai
20010900	ERCO Lichtbericht	Lüdenscheid
20010901	GQ Japan 2001 9月号	Tokyo
20010901	PJ仙台マガジン9月号	Sendai
20010901	仙台市政だより9月号	Sendai
20010909	河北新報	Sendai
20010913	週刊新潮	Tokyo
20010921	GAアーキテクト	Tokyo
20010922	よみうりCha! 10月号	Tokyo
20011001	地方自治コンピュータ10月号	Tokyo
20011002	せんだいメディアテーク写真集	Tokyo
20011002	日経流通新聞	Tokyo
20011011	河北新報	Sendai
20011012	河北新報	Sendai
20011015	月刊ミュゼ	Tokyo
20011019	河北新報	Sendai
20011024	図書館の学校	Tokyo
20011024	河北新報	Sendai
20011025	朝日新聞	Tokyo
20011026	Diatxt. ダイアテキスト05	Kyoto
20011026	河北新報	Sendai
20011031	毎日新聞	Tokyo
20011031	産経新聞	Tokyo
20011031	読売新聞	Tokyo
20011031	ニュースレターSURF	Sendai
20011031	河北新報	Sendai
200110	ドコモレジャーマップ	Sendai
200110	spike(free paper)	
200110	伊達人 秋季号	Sendai
20011100	selco セルコ	Sendai
20011101	Begin 2000 11	Tokyo
20011109	河北新報	Sendai
20011114	インテリアタイムス	Tokyo
20011115	はなやま	Sendai
20011120	広告特集アルファ情報館	Sendai
20011121	せんだいタウン情報	Sendai
20011121	図書館の学校	Tokyo
20011123	この街に暮らす（住宅情報東北版特別編集）	Tokyo
200111	第1回仙台国際音楽コンクール報告書	Sendai
20011201	Esquire(エスクァイア日本版)	Tokyo
20011201	relax 58	Tokyo
20011201	仙台市政だより	Sendai
20011201	東北経済産業情報東北21	Sendai
20011201	旅	Tokyo
20011205	せんだいタウン情報	Sendai
20011205	友の栞	Sendai
20011205	デザインの現場	Tokyo
20011207	ウィークリー・オーレ	Sendai
20011208	河北新報	Sendai
20011210	デザインニュース	Tokyo
20011210	LIVES-MT	
20011210	デザインニュース	Tokyo
20011210	河北新報	Sendai
20011211	N2W エヌツーダブリュ	Nagoya
20011212	河北新報	Sendai
20011214	全国公文協通信	Tokyo
20011215	仙台市政だより青葉区版あおば	Sendai
20011216	朝日新聞	Tokyo
20011219	せんだいタウン情報	Sendai
20011221	仙台支部だより	Sendai
20011225	ロジマガ	Sendai
20011225	ロジマガ	Sendai
20011225	視聴覚教育時報	Tokyo
20011225	エンセン	Sendai
20011228	りらく	Sendai
200112	河北新報	Sendai
2001	毎日新聞	Tokyo
2001	東北ざいむ	Sendai
2001	ぱるみやぎ	Sendai
2001	6年社会科学習資料/わたしたちのくらしと税金	Sendai
2001	2001仙台市職員募集ガイド	Sendai
20020101	社会教育	Tokyo
20020101	ブレーン	Tokyo
20020101	仙台市政だより	Sendai
20020101	日本経済新聞	Tokyo
20020101	芸術新潮	Tokyo
20020101	河北ウィークリー	Sendai
20020102	せんだいタウン情報	Sendai
20020102	せんだいタウン情報	Sendai
20020107	日経アーキテクチュア	Tokyo
20020116	せんだいタウン情報	Sendai
20020126	よみうりCha!	Tokyo
20020128	ライトニング	Tokyo
20020128	りらく	Sendai
20020128	朝日新聞	Tokyo
20020129	河北新報	Sendai
200201	l'architecture d'aujourd'hui	Paris
200201	伊達人	Sendai
200201	ユア・ビジネス	Tokyo
20020201	杜の伝言版ゆるる	Sendai
20020201	AXIS	Tokyo
20020201	AXIS	Tokyo
20020205	河北新報夕刊平成14年2月5日	Sendai
20020205	伊達人冬季号2002. Vol.36	Sendai
20020205	伊達人春季号2002. Vol.37	Sendai
20020205	朝日新聞	Sendai
20020215	月刊Newsがわかる	Tokyo
20020215	月刊Ｎｅｗｓがわかる2002　2	Tokyo
20020218	毎日新聞	Tokyo
20020219	AXIS	Tokyo
20020220	河北新報	Sendai
20020221	河北新報	Sendai
20020222	PROJECT48 http://www.a-matter.com	Munich
20020228	河北新報	Sendai
20020301	家庭画報	Tokyo
20020301	ソトコト	Tokyo
20020301	美術手帖	Tokyo
20020301	平成13年度文部科学省民間社会教育活動振興費補助事業報告書 生涯学習年報(Link)	Tokyo
20020306	月刊CHINTAI東北版	Tokyo
20020318	河北新報 夕刊	Sendai
20020318	河北新報	Sendai
20020330	シニアとパソコンが社会を元気にするおもしろい話	Tokyo
20020330	offer	Takaoka
20020330	府中市彫刻のあるまちづくりシリーズ17	Tokyo
20020331	仙台市社会学級研究会だより杜	Sendai
200203	C/P Culture Pocket	Osaka
200203	伊達人	Sendai

Sendai Mediatheque

Client Sendai City

Architects Toyo Ito & Associates, Architects: Toyo Ito, Tatsuo Kuwahara, Takeo Higashi, Makoto Yokomizo, Toyohiko Kobayashi, Shinichi Takeuchi, Takuhiro Seo, Hironori Matsubara, Reo Yokota

Structural engineer Sasaki Structural Consultants: Mutsuro Sasaki, Masahiro Ikeda, Shuji Tada, Akira Suzuki

Lighting Lighting Planners Associates: Kaoru Mende, Hiroyasu Shoji

Services engineer:

  Air-conditioning ES Associates: Eiji Sato, Hisakatsu Hemmi

  Sanitary services Sogo Consultants: Haruo Atsumi, Hiroyuki Ogawa

  Electrical engineer Ohtaki E&M Consulting Office: Makiyo Ohtaki, Seiji Matsumoto + Sogo Consultants: Futao Endo, Koji Iida

Acoustic Nagata Acoustics: Chiaki Ishiwata + Nittobo Acoutic Engineering CO., LTD. (Studio Theater on the 7th floor): Motoyuki Sakai

Disaster prevention consultant Ataka Fire Safety Design Office: Kiyoshi Suzuki + Nippon Steel Corporation (fireproof planning): Masahi Takayama + Akeno Corporation (fireproof screen on the 6th floor): Hideo Nakajima

Signage planning workshop for architecture and urbanism (direction): Akira Suzuki, Akira Imafuji + Matsuda Office / Ushiwakamaru (graphic design): Yukimasa Matsuda

Furniture Karim Rashid Inc. (1st, 5th and 6th floors) + Kazuyo Sejima & Associates (2nd floor): Kazuyo Sejima, Yoshitaka Tanase + K. T. Architecture (3rd and 4th floors): Yoshiaki Tezuka, Hirono Koike + Studio X (7th floor): Ross Lovegrove

Information system planning Mitsubishi Reserch Institute, Inc.: Hideyuki Morita, Itaru Jinbo

Wearable sign Kosuke Tsumura

General contractors Kumagai Takenaka Ando Hashimoto JV

Design phase April 1995 to August 1997
Construction December 1997 to August 2000
Site area 3948.72 m^2
Building area 2933.12 m^2
Total floor area 21,682.15 m^2
Building coverage ratio 74.28 % (limit: 100 %)
Floor area ratio 497.73 % (limit: 500 %)
Building height 36.49 m (eaves height: 31.8 m)
Total cost ¥ 12,466,650,000

Publisher Actar
Editor Tomoko Sakamoto
in collaboration with Albert Ferré
Graphic design Sandra Neumaier
Photographs and image credits
Ramon Prat: page 2, 6, 39 (center), 72, 75, 78, 80, 86, 88, 92-99, 104-110, 116-188
Tomio Ohashi: page 14, 40
Toyo Ito & Associates, Architects, 000studio and Ryoji Ikeda: pages 26-29
Makoto Yokomizo: pages 42-45
Dana Buntrock: page 62
Toyo Ito & Architects Associates, Sasaki Structural Consultants, Sendai Mediatheque, Lighting Planners
Associates, Matsuda Office, Karim Rashid Inc., Kazuyo Sejima & Associates, K. T. Architecture, Studio X
Translation Actar, Alfred Birnbaum (page 7 / From "Sendai Mediatheque Report: Under Construction")
Text editing Anna Tetas, Elaine Fradley
Production collaborators Carmen Galán, Oriol Rigat, bylea
Printing Ingoprint SA
Distribution Actar
Roca i Batlle, 2
08023 Barcelona. Spain
Tel: +34 93 418 77 59
Fax: +34 93 418 67 07
info@actar-mail.com
www.actar.es

Printed and bound in the EU
Barcelona, May 2003